D0796941

DISCARDED FROM
GARFIELD COUNTY
LIBRARIES

Garfield County Libraries
Rifle Branch Library
107 E. 2nd Street
Rifle, CO 81650
(970) 625-3471 Fax (970) 625-3549
www.garfieldlibraries.org

Also by Bin Ramke

The Difference between Night and Day

White Monkeys

The Language Student

The Erotic Light of Gardens

Massacre of the Innocents

Wake

Airs, Waters, Places

Matter

Tendril

Theory of Mind
New & Selected Poems

Theory of Mind
New & Selected Poems

Bin Ramke

OMNIDAWN PUBLISHING
RICHMOND, CALIFORNIA
2009

© Bin Ramke 2009. All rights reserved.

Cover Image: Gerard Richter, German born 1932,
Little Landscape by the Sea, 1969, oil on canvas, 28½ x 41⅜ inches.
Through prior gift of Mr. and Mrs. Lewis Larned Coburn;
Gift of Lannan Foundation. 1997.171, The Art Institute of Chicago.
Photography © The Art Institute of Chicago.
Courtesy: Marian Goodman Gallery, New York.

Book cover and interior design by Ken Keegan.

Offset printed in the United States on archival, acid-free recycled paper
by Thomson-Shore, Inc., Dexter, Michigan

Omnidawn Publishing is committed to preserving ancient
forests and natural resources. We elected to print this title on
30% postconsumer recycled paper, processed chlorine-free. As
a result, for this printing, we have saved:

4 Trees (40' tall and 6-8" diameter)
1,752 Gallons of Wastewater
1 million BTUs of Total Energy
106 Pounds of Solid Waste
364 Pounds of Greenhouse Gases

Omnidawn Publishing made this paper choice because our
printer, Thomson-Shore, Inc., is a member of Green Press
Initiative, a nonprofit program dedicated to supporting authors,
publishers, and suppliers in their efforts to reduce their use of
fiber obtained from endangered forests.

For more information, visit www.greenpressinitiative.org

Environmental impact estimates were made using the Environmental Defense
Paper Calculator. For more information visit: www.edf.org/papercalculator

Library of Congress Catalog-in-Publication Data
Ramke, Bin, 1947-
    Theory of mind : new & selected poems / Bin Ramke.
        p. cm.
    ISBN 978-1-890650-41-4 (pbk. : alk. paper)
    I. Title.
    PS3568.A446T47 2009
    811'.54--dc22

                                                    2009030462

Published by Omnidawn Publishing, Richmond, California
www.omnidawn.com   (510) 237-5472   (800) 792-4957
            10 9 8 7 6 5 4 3 2 1

        ISBN: 978-1-890650-41-4

for Linda

and for Nic, Mary, Rick, and Julie

CONTENTS

When we view interactions through the lens of social cognition, even mundane events become magnificent in their complexity…Through neurocognitive abilities and knowledge of social and interpersonal situations, we construct ideas about people's dispositions and thoughts. This process is known by the rather abstract name "Theory of Mind."
—Michael Foster Green

Dwells with me still mine irksome *Memory*,
Which, both to keepe, and lose, grieves equally
—John Donne, *Heroicall Epistle*

Anomalies of Water

Water

Is one way of putting it
About the whole world, a gliding
Singular element of

Fruit, knowledge, names, hazards of desire
                    —Vicki Hearne, "So There Is Justice"

WHAT ONCE WAS LOST IS LOST AGAIN

My beautiful umbrella, the one that folds
and can be carried in the pocket so un-
obtrusive, my friend from that other life,

we are we are made of wounds! that scar
that used to be above my right eye,
that vision that smell that small

death that shoe that lace that aglet
that raincoat that hat that bundle
on the train that memory

For the trumpet rhimes are sound bound, soar more and the like.
For the Shawm rhimes are lawn fawn moon boon and the like.

That man that peace that death. I was able
to make sounds and to live among sounds
the train would swirl the noise of its engine

as it pushed through the tunnel the mountains
it made big sounds which bounced back
and back again and delighted itself its riders

I need my umbrella the rain will come again
the sounds of rain the sundry

For every word has its marrow
in the English tongue for order and for delight.

For I have lost my umbrella and water descends from
Old English *clūd* mass of rock or earth, related to clot,

clouded the days and delightful, the thunder.

"WHAT DID YOU MAKE THE CLOUDS OUT OF?"

Deeply she makes what she makes
the artist makes her distress out of clouds
this story in the wind and a cloud
and the children know they are stories.
What did you make the children out of?
Clouds consume themselves like children or
the wind does what wind will, and wells itself
up out of ocean; then
she made her story her

child: consider the bee,
Apis mellifera, which makes its young
out of wax, little Galateas busy busy
I am honey for you, Dear,
she makes what she makes
a distress of clouds a storm a kind of wealth
the golden architecture of honey, of hive
glitters in the dark, the humid dark a mind
not of bee but of honey, of golden hive;
a child entomologist
knows crawling and flying as options
watch small things loving

want bees of my own, and honey
and wax that would be world
I could make in that world clouds
of wax and a sky of honey and flora
and fauna of wings and
bees do love me and are honey for me
and make babies of wax which come to life come
home and immortal as the hive the
swarm which is a cloud stinging.

CUSTODY OF THE EYES

Where they paint porch ceilings a shade
of blue you see on good days as if
through to sky two years after the storms
a land is streaked with blue, plastic under
which roof and rafter remain erased. Remains

my dream, by the sea, the slow warm sea
its own dream a geometry
all of an evening. Water.

There was a way there then to read which took
some small effort and cost an evening.
She would and he would. Then they together.
Such little things we were then, creatures
of the summer sea. Waking

But a puddle of water no more than one finger deep,
lying between the stones upon a paved street, offers a view
downwards under the earth to as great a reach as the open
heavens yawn on high, so that you seem to look down upon
the clouds and heaven, and you see manifest objects
miraculously buried beneath the earth.
(Lucretius, *De Rerum Natura*)

We paused beside the pools that lie
Under the forest bough,
Each seemed as 'twere a little sky
Gulfed in a world below;
A firmament of purple light
Which in the dark earth lay.
(Shelley, "To Jane: The Recollection")

We love the light, or would, we wash ourselves
in it, it kills. The water is a form of light
heavy and within it the glitter
lingers dully but is there, is there
like earth itself waiting its turn.

Where there is no doubt there is no judgment
(Wittgenstein, "On Certainty")

Looking down the boy did drown
his future in the gutter he crossed. He smiled.
Looking down he saw himself as in a pool
he leaped across, a wet inversion
and would have stopped mid leap to see
himself below look up his glance.
And then it was gone the face the moment
the boy looked back but missed the glitter
the moment passed. A fiftieth part of a second
is roughly a moment. Or less.

There is a way water can be thought to live,
to make just demands, to judge.
Fanciful water. Only surface, all the way
down. Watery in

that land the damage
remains and rounds its edges, soothes
the woundedness which is
one way. The other being
to look to see.

A SORT OF DROWNING, A SLOWER DANCE

It is the way horses appear to walk, that one toe
delicately picks a place to step or once we walked
my child and me down sixth avenue and heard
an eerie chorus arising around us of breath
the breathing behind cardboard of men and women
asleep it was late were walking home from the subway

I live here none can keep me away from home
some die at home and would call it good except
they are dead and cannot call. The disappointing dead.

To watch fish from above look down into the water
and make no threatening shadow

a way to move in the world to make
no shadow. To kiss. To move
mouth against mouth.

If it is a forest there are mounded movements
of limbs in the wind and are paths
between limbs where air insinuates and birds
and a kindness of chlorophyll accumulates
as if waiting for us to pass as if waiting for
a time to come when the greenness will be
complete. "Forest" means incomplete.
A placing of the foot delicately between.

THE TWELVE SYMMETRIES

1 *Was It What It Was*

I walked up all your stars, stairs to wake you, walk you home but
you were not there where the taking, talking, was taking place,
taking the place of, the pace of a love affair, afar, a fair love and
languor, language will do that; Rise, balloon. Blue balloon.
We are not to fall together, each falls apart apart from the other—
an asymptote a kind of self, selfish kind. A clinging.

2 *Later There Was*

Inclined this way, the head is zero-shaped and tightly filled with
memory. As a child I was terrified
a balloon might burst at my lips, the sound
would deafen me; the concussion a kind of rage released...

after the party, little deflated splashes, color on the floor,
also cake crumbs and sticky
remains, the breath of the mother the décor of the day.

3 *So He Was*

Naturally naïve I believed the balloon bursting would release
the secret I had whispered too loudly blowing it up, someone listening.

4 *Paper*

She and I will rise burning paper, paper
burning us rising. It will be a trap a trip

us too making out of paper and paste a balloon of our scraps
those letters those poems

Burn it up, we said, laughing as blisters formed.

O, furious balloon, with words. Of. O.

5   *Cures for the Cynic*

That O quickly fills or empties a catastrophe of zero...take my life for
instance, emptying and filling like any old bathtub. Or yours. A circular
tub, an agony of porcelain

"Here doe I see a Cynick housed in his Tub,
scorning all wealth and state."
Water fills
water fills it furiously. It furiously fills.

*The remedy of dis-
contentment; or, a
treatise of contentation
in whatsoever condition.*
Bishop Joseph Hall, 1645

6   *Categories*

The basic symmetries of the Lie are four: Lies of Shame, of Disgrace,
Lies of Need and Lies of Comfort. Each of these engages metaphor,
irony, and poetry. Or, Self, Other, and Us. Or, the lie is a common friend,
full of foreboding but willing to hold your hand in the dark hours
when bright anxieties await just beyond the corners which need turning.

7   *She Said*

This is not to say, she said, that I forgive you. She said this unhooking
an item of clothing. It was a small item, nothing that would be noticed
but by one who understood the nature of need, the kind of need he would
feed on, self-cannibalizing need which required at all cost to be covered
by some sort of clothing, some small wisp which could be secretly
hooked into place while no one, or she, was looking.

8   *Group Theory*

The tetrahedron, too, has twelve symmetries.

9   *Restrictions*

What One Must Not Touch: baby birds, fallen,
the emulsion side of the film,
oneself, others, delicate objects,
delicate subjects, dangerous objects,
open sores, close-friends' children,
the children of strangers, the actual
eyeball, the exposed interior.

10   *Truth*

A casual survey taken of his own erotic fantasies left him quivering.
For no one can bear his own her own despair sexually embodied.
No body can bear its own weight but will soon and seriously reject
symmetry, all mirrors turning opaque,
all echo silenced.

11   *What It Will Become*

My breath is continuous and dimensionless,
"Dimension," being simply what is needed, the space
within which you can show what it is, whatever
it is; for instance: I have a balloon in three dimensions
whose surface is in two: I drew her face on my balloon,
tears in her eyes and mine.
During the night my breath did escape—
a whisper from her throat, my Love's, a dream at some distance.

All day I said goodbye and then I failed to leave. The lie was uncertain; was in the not leaving or was it the saying itself?

THERE ARE SEVEN MANNERS OF LOVING

what gives the soul its deepest wounds brings to it best relief
—Beatrijs of Nazareth

A useful concept, "soul," similar to the square root
of minus one. Ah, utility. She breathed upon me
and I did wake.
             When the boy was a boy he woke
one morning and was no longer young but still
a boy.
     What to do with such a moment is the soul.
The word means only itself and is a manner of loving,
the first. The second is this: one morning the boy
awoke and was young again, and laughed at nothing
and nothing laughed back at him and spoke.

The third manner of loving is death.

The fourth manner of loving is when the first bird
of the morning visits your feeder and morning glory
gleams in the rising heat even before the sun
and the dew of the morning hisses into vapor
and from your window you watch afraid but
still you stand there and a life a …

No there is no fourth manner.

A fifth manner of loving is to wait in half-light half-
your life and count the small winged bodies which gather
on the window sill. Your cat will come to you and whisper

in her way, and she will look as though she is looking
at you, but really you do know the love of the world
is in the small flickers of her tail which have to do
with anything but you, have to do with the history
of the mitochondria, with the shape of proteins well-folded
and with the many molecules floating into your vision
some translation out of a nice, small century past.

26

A sixth manner of loving is to climb into the family you have
and hold onto any scrap of them which remains after the floods
and the simple storms which break things—the breaking
of things is the world but is also its manner of loving
which is horror and we thought we had moved past
this error which is the presentness of the world which kills
us, which is disease and famine and flood and others
you know the list it is the soul of the world but
when the people and the place you came from are flooded
and scattered and the last of your uncles lies
in a suburb of Dallas breathing through a machine
that is alas the seventh manner of loving. Praise.

The water which comes with the storm
and fills the small valleys and the houses
of the people is a love, but is not a manner
of loving. The thingness of the water is
beyond us, is us, is in us already. We die
of it, true, but any wound wavers.

WAS IT FALLEN IT WAS A FLOATING WORLD

Along the dangerous canals the storm found its way
and when the trees obeyed they grew
too much to bear to bare those leaves
descending slowly at first then slowly later

wind will intensely its tense engagement raise
with limbs of trees and an occasional human
to walk himself home no man walked

willingly, with the wind, all against, the women
were likewise walking in the natural order:
leaves falling,

trees falling, winds rising. Child, she, smaller
than most, skirted the littered streets
when it was over, the storm, the fall, the fanciful there.

Isaiah 51:16   And I have put my words in thy mouth,
and I have covered thee in the shadow of mine hand,
that I may plant the heavens, and lay the foundations of the earth

And then trees dismayed displayed
too much too bare; the leaves descended slowly
at first then slowly later.

Wind does rise to break little limbs of these
occasional walkers, humans hoping themselves home.
None walk with the wind, all against. Aghast

men and women provoke (invoking) the natural order: leaves fail,
trees fall, winds revise. Engaged as witness, she, smaller
than most, skirted the littered streets past

the storm, fell into a felicitous *here* where
Martin Heidegger who is dead once said:
"man is world-forming" and you know,

somebody had to; and he further said "the stone
is worldless" and he said "the animal is poor in world"
but Heidegger devotes his body to ideas

but consider the driest of animals
a lizard on a flat rock a world
for the wanderer. World forming, *Consider*,
from *con* plus *sider*, star like constellation, a kind
of world. The alternative *were* and

world, old, old man worldly, were
and weary, an etymology…
fluffy world, soft soft softer.

It was fallen; was it a floating world?

Sleep on a hard bed, but a bed. Or rather, a narrow realm
of anguish, and sleep as a bitter residue of waking, a place,
a placement, a kind of depositing—deposit as in precipitate—
a life a precipitate of events and attitudes and biology.

Using small automated telescopes in Arizona and Hawaii,
the HATNet project has detected an object transiting one
member of the double star system ADS 16402 AB…
This system is a pair of G0 main-sequence stars. The planet,
designated HAT-P-1b, appears to be at least as large
in radius, and smaller in mean density,
than any previously-known planet.

That it is both the largest and the least dense of the nearly
two hundred worlds so far found outside our system, and
that it orbits one of a pair of stars in the constellation Lacerta,
(*Lacerta*: a small and inconspicuous northern constellation
(the Lizard), on the edge of the Milky Way
between Cygnus and Andromeda
about 450 light-years from Earth),
makes it a likely candidate for Heaven.

"This new planet, if you could imagine putting it in a cosmic water glass, it would float"

Robert Noyes, Smithsonian Astrophysical Observatory

Here? Hereafter.

Geology in Astronomy, each
planet precipitated itself out of its early self, each was once
light or wet and now grows dark or dense

early 16th cent.: from Latin *praecipitat- 'thrown headlong,'* from
the verb *praecipitare,* from *praeceps, praecip(it)- 'headlong,'* from
prae 'before' + *caput 'head.'* The original sense of the verb was
hurl down, send violently.

*I find that I lose my patience lately and I am up and down with
my emotions. Yesterday was a dark day and I just cried off and on.
I don't know if I am depressed or if this is just a combination of
still healing from my surgeries, not enough sleep, my ovaries
being gone, etc. I'm tired of going to see doctors every week and
just want to be left alone. Has anyone else experienced this
type of feeling?* (a string, an internet help site, just
a person asking. Just asking.)

If we are the angelic order then where what pillowed world will take us
and will it float again against the wind, a balloon of my own, or your
exhaled breath, kept and shaped this way, dangerously soft and billowed

but look, her skirt in the light breeze, her hair in the updraft, her breath
in the cold air a light behind and the boundaries broken, soft escape.

LIES

asleep
in the next room with
a balloon above her head—
a dotted-line balloon—
a non-Euclidean space
which contains her
dream, which is
—I wish it were—

the balloon is empty, or,
her dream lies
around her,
an empty thought-balloon
to indicate the past,
its pure O of elegance.

How to make Balloones, also the Morter Peece to discharge them…
Into this Balloone you may put Rockets,
Serpents, Starres, Fiends, Petards.
Bate, Mysteries of Nature & Art, 1634

Any bursting a violence.
Inclined this way, the head is balloon-shaped
tightly filled with memory.

I was terrified a balloon would burst
at my lips, the sound would deafen me;
the concussion a rage released…

after the party, little deflated splashes
of color on the floor, also cake crumbs
and the sticky remains,
the breath of the mother decorating the day.

Symmetry is the chance to return
to initial conditions…not nostalgia,
just home; not home but humility,

the humiliation of symmetry plain and
periodic agony not agony but a ghostly monotony

behind the arras a mother not uncle, standing
breast forward awaiting a blade and a piercing peaceful

as desperation in a phone booth
when phone booths were soundproof
when there were phone booths and the desperate would
make calls from there late in life or at night home
hoping Mom would answer, Dad already asleep.

106. *Suppose some adult had told a child that he had been on the moon. The child tells me the story, and I say it was only a joke, the man hadn't been on the moon; no one has ever been on the moon; the moon is a long way off and it is impossible to climb up there or fly there.—If now the child insists, saying perhaps there is a way of getting there which I don't know, etc. what reply could I make to him? What reply could I make to the adults of a tribe who believe that people sometimes go to the moon (perhaps that is how they interpret their dreams), and who indeed grant that there are no ordinary means of climbing up to it or flying there? —But a child will not ordinarily stick to such a belief and will soon be convinced by what we tell him seriously.*

121. *Can one say: "Where there is no doubt there is no knowledge either"?*

160. *The child learns by believing the adult. Doubt comes after belief.*
                                        —Wittgenstein, *On Certainty*

HOW IT FEELS, AND WHY

For There Was No Rain in Paradise
…Because of the Delicate Construction of the Spiritual Herbs and Flowers.
Christopher Smart

Visceral pain tends to be felt in the region of skin supplied by
the same nerves (as this relates to the embryological position
of the developing organ, the pain can be referred distantly—

She did cut less deep she did to herself sometimes
deeply. She a child who saw through, mirrored
clearly and cut deeply into her self, her proof. She did

e.g. heart pain to the shoulders, appendix pain to the navel,
and in men testicular pain to the upper abdomen). Localization
of pain on the skin is probably aided by touch information,
and perhaps even prior expectation.

I placed a hand in the fire to hold the molecules
which would speed past, into flesh, fly, the flaying
of my own skin a self, my proof. I have.

Pain can undergo a large degree of *descending control*.
The main source of inhibition of pain signals is the
periaqueductal grey matter (PAG) in the midbrain,
which projects both upwards and downwards, and releases
enkephalin and other endogenous opioids.

For the malignancy of fire is oweing to the Devil's
hiding of light, till it became visible darkness.
Any, a pain-induced pity. Piety no pity.

She did cut less deep she did to herself sometimes
deeply. She was a child and saw through her mirror
clearly and cut deeply into her self, her proof. She did.

Pit or pith, or what is the word for that whiteness
beneath orange, beneath the peel? Albedo. A measure
of light, of the moon or any surface, such as her face

in the malignant mirror smiling miraculous, dear.
Back at her face Latin *facies* form, appearance, face.

The flowers would die of it, the rain harsh harshly falling
the storm the stirred air pressing. It stirs us.

A Theory of Narrative

The problem, according to Bháskara: of a flock of geese
ten times the square root of the flock departed for the Mánasa Lake
at the approach of a cloud

sensory nerves enter the cord through the *dorsal roots,*
with cell bodies lying within the *dorsal root ganglia.*
There is one root for each vertebra, and the distribution
of each across the surface of the body is a *dermatome*

an eighth part went to a forest of St'halapadminis

these form bands down the body, with some distortion
across the limbs and the abdomen. Damage to a spinal nerve
causes loss of light touch sensation

three couples were engaged in sport on the water
which abounds in the delicate fibers of lotus

Tell, Dear, the number of the flock.

So if ten times the square root of the number,
plus an eighth of the number, plus six, is what we know
even if never has she known the delicious terror
of a cloud approaching Mánasa Lake,
even if she has never known how to be half
of a couple sporting on the surface of water

34

she can know the square of twelve, a hundred
forty four geese and the sound they make makes
loud accounting. The cloud could bring rain
which frightens the delicate, is a danger and dark.

Fibers carrying pain terminate in *Rexed laminae* 1 and 2
(layers 2 and 3 are the *substantia gelatinosa*); proprioceptive and
touch fibers penetrate through all six layers, sending collaterals
to the deeper layers before ascending in the ipsilateral *dorsal column.*

Natural History of Flight

To Cher Ami the *Croix de Guerre* awarded for delivering twelve
messages in wartime in spite of wounds. From late Latin *pipio(n-,) young
cheeping bird,* imitative in origin, *Pigeon* appears twice in the King James
translation. More properly Rock Dove, but Pigeon will do. A bird of the
city has adopted us, and loves, in her way, us, as a kind of truth. Leviticus
12:6: she shall bring a lamb of the first year for a burnt offering, and a
young pigeon, or a turtledove, for a sin offering.

…cortical processing seems to involve increasing sensitivity to particular
types of stimuli, with increasingly large receptive fields. However, the
nature of this processing *may* be oriented towards representations of
objects as things that can be interacted with.…

Isaiah 7: 18 And it shall come to pass in that day,
[that] the lord shall hiss for the fly in the uttermost
part of the rivers of Egypt,
and for the bee in the land of Assyria…the only
appearance of bee in the Bible…

How much an area of skin is represented on the primary
sensory cortex changes depending on how much that area is used
for fine touch discrimination, and how dense the receptors are—
hence…the enlarged digit fields of Braille readers, and the decreasing field
when use of a finger is blocked experimentally

I wish to speak of the bees... honey-flies...

The fact that the hive contains so much that is wonderful
does not warrant our seeking to add to its wonders. Besides,
I myself have now for a long time ceased to look for anything
more beautiful in this world, or more interesting, than the
truth; or at least than the effort one is able to make toward
the truth. (Maeterlinck, *The Life of the Bee*)

Pain projection is less straightforward than touch or proprioception,
is less well understood. Perception of pain can be altered by many things.
For there was no rain in Paradise because of the delicate construction
of the spiritual herbs and flowers.

ASK, TASK, SIGN, ASSIGN

To the task of repairing the spider's web with your fingers,
add trisecting the angle using only origami.

Assigned the task of solving a string of quadratic equations
while listening to the hydrogen bonds breaking, she whistled an
imitation.

Asked to sign the small drawing, the artist wrote a famous equation
in the lower right-hand corner. We had heard rumors of this silverpoint
miracle on watercolor paper.

I continued to breathe in spite of a pewter gleam in the sky,
a green swirl of lake beneath. Such a day is its own category,
accused by wind and water.

A further sign of drought is the breakage of glass distinctly if
distantly heard when the coefficients contract and the calculations wind
down doll-like, the keys in their backs slower revolving than planets.

The despair the artist feels faced with a non-distributive
algebra reminds me of the cycloid Galileo studied by weighing the
area under the arc to find it was three times the area of the circle.
He made models of metal, poured liquid into molds. I understand
less now than ever, and rejoice like angels.

COLD SONNETS

Evil Days, Careful Nights

"Care" as curiosity: is there a better word
for sin than careless—feel the lack of sun a
chlorophilia, green beneath heraldry
the snow—the flesh gone missing for months
the wish for short skirts, for burning;

the third wish, the life
as you live it is one wish. The second
is dreaming—real dreams, sleep,
not that silliness of wistful wishing.
Satan and Death and Sin Intervening.

The wishes. "Divide eight into two parts
such that their product multiplied by their
difference comes to as much as possible,
proving everything" Ferrari

———

demanded of Tartaglia (1548)

taking care to confound: caretaking
is a modern mode: who speaks keeps
calm, so carefully if I spoke to her
would she care? She did not answer
and cannot dare. Grieve, lament,

and sickbed are what parts of speech?
But my answer does not cure me, care
as I might. The one who suffers is
the one who speaks; lie next to her
in her sickbed careless of cost—

first the pillows then the body cools.
As I walked past the wooded park sounds
of birds or of swings in the playground.

⁓

A short transparent dress, (after Anne Carson)
a word in Sappho, somewhere now unknown no
knowing the sound and the signature molecular

a word meant that once and one was in her son
the song not ever heard by the now

living, and could she read? Pollux: *beudos*. No,
more, shining through. A surface shatters
light, "transparent" is process a shatter

a shuddering short dress unworn or unbearable
any unwearable dress erotic error (too cold)
any word heard: *kimberikon*. Dazzle through

fabric, the glint, obliquely sliding sleeve.

KNOWING BETTER

In some past a person of learning and poetry believed
migrating birds spent winters on the moon…
Aristotle argued they sleep under mud of marshes
and the big ones gave rides to the little.

Nocturnal migrants inspire a desire to know
the arts of the birds and the pleasures of the fishes.

Our cities are invaded by: our shadows,
our pets, our intentions, our errors, our children;
our cities identical to selves, our pastures
are the shadows of our cities. The history contained
in this language contrary, contrite
response to the damage we do and did and will.

We do destroy ourselves daily
and dream it away every night
to watch such shadow-birds fly moonward;

the land is the land, and home.
The water is water, and home.
The light is the light is the light
and is home to itself.

Quick sparrows over the snow
a lone a long voice a calling
and the particles of longing
design and time click on
ward as it as if an element
al desire clicks onward as if

but things to do are not done
a light dragged unwilling against
the hooked night encroaching
dispersed—no those

are sparrows passing, not
hours, not ours, birds grow
symbolic only if you let them.
Quit quickly, inside to warm,
imagine the pleasures.

CAJUN, A CORRUPTION OF "ARCADIAN," OR OF A MI'KMAWI'SIMK TERM FOR "FULLNESS"

I am often confused by the words "equal" and "between." To say one thing is another thing is like saying…one thing. And what separates them. There were several major storms in my past, and then there were two, separately named, which killed three-fourths of the trees of New Orleans. The trees of the Gulf Coast will continue decaying into the atmosphere, little particles of tree dancing into the air, carbon mainly, and even my mother's body will be little particles in the earth and then air and there will be rains thus into earth again. The French who made a life with the help of the Mi'kmaq were dispersed into the colonies. Ethnic cleansing. Clean air. Clean water. Clean land.

MAKE THEM CRY

The cloudy nuance of home every husk
to eat his way out of, tunneling his own skin
and so leaving, his luggage trails in dust
(little wheels bounce; butterflies frolic along
this path his road to away a way like Tao
a new beginning (unlike the unliked old

beginnings clouds of butterflies wheel beside
him clever and various, veined, visible: between veins
of a butterfly's wing veiled as a bride, nubile
beneath the sheathe of the shade of home—
not home, now he, he comes a way, shadowy.
Eating earth, the earth.

⁓

Doki-Doki Majo Shinpan, the girl-touching adventure
game that SNK Playmore released for Nintendo DS on
July 5 translates to "[thump-thump of a heartbeat] Witch
Judgment"; you play a boy who has to determine whether
a girl is a witch by touching parts of her body she wears
a halter, it is summer, she squirms embarrassedly.

Dear Students and Members of Mynderse Academy
and Surround Towns, This petition is to help in the
stopping of Anthony P_____'s advancement towards
any girl that moves. Whether he touches them or
tickles them…it needs to be stopped. Please sign this
petition and tell your friends. This is a
growing matter that needs to be controlled.

⁓

When the Supreme Personality of Godhead Krishna was so ordered by
His mother, He immediately opened His mouth just like an ordinary boy.
Then mother Yasoda saw within that mouth the complete opulence of
creation. (Sudarsana)

———

Imagine the worm, how it slides through and slides through
earth, a tube engorging and disgorging the very earth itself. And birds
do breathe when flying, I'm sure of it, through air their bodies glide
and into and out of their bodies the air. Clever. Fish. Water. What else?

The story was that Krishna's friend told on him, that he was eating dirt,
so even the gods were children once and petty, gliding through human
gliding through time (no foundations only nets…not through but
within among—not time but whatever caused him to say "time" and

think "death") looking into the sarcophagal mouth of the planet, miner
and milk-drinker, otherwise known as boy or girl, sex
a tube equally available tunnel known as sex through which
not through always in into she tunnels he tunnels an old
word…

I am here on an errand on earth the Green Knight said
to Gawain. Old word, *eorth*, old place, old old. Errand.

THINGS CAN BE DONE THE BODY

can be sewn shut
opened
caressed
controlled
cured

it can be sewed and sawed
swallowed it can swoon be
sworn at

can it be doubled
replicated
repeated child father child
daughter sister mother sister
daughter

it can be sewn to itself

and what can it contain
a self
a surgery
all handiwork
a length of intestine
inte stinum
a handful of item

and what is doubled
twin   DNA
mirrored
misery misery
mystery some
initiated mysticism

drawn upon it can
be decorated it
can be scarified
can be painted pained

it can be closed with pins
with thread it can open

This is what bodies do
and why, why not flag the
mutilation of summer by wearing
something old
by warring against the re
pressed as
the trees lose leaves this way,
sere and flammable.

My own mother did it, everyone's
did and does. It will not kill us.

Something will, mothers cannot be
blamed like weather can breathing
as a chore a charring
of the lungs this way
and that, the trees alight in the distance
in the wind waving
needles threading.

THE MAXIMUM OF SPARROWS
INSTANTANEOUSLY COUNTABLE

Five, let us say, beneath the table around our feet, you recount
the feeling it gave you to see the girl in the green dress walking her dog
her spaghetti-straps also green she carried a little bag of shit. *The whole
world of things actual and possible*, Russell wrote. Actual and possible
and green. *A bliss in proof and prov'd.*

One sparrow flying splashed faeces on my face, my lips. I had a napkin handy.

Map.

The girl and the green dress are gone.

A crowd of sparrows flew over me and my table. I do not know
the number—I could guess (twelve?) but there is no truth to be
known, no point. *Mappa mundi.*

It felt wet, as if a raindrop, a harbinger.

Why love the word "sparrow," *passer*. At an instant, at hand.
We see three, and two, in a moment together.   (*Subitus*, sudden knowledge)

LUSTROUS DEMONSTRATION
(Clyfford Still)

His father tied his feet lowered him headfirst
into the well to check the cracked casing he could see

Behold, I stand by the well of water; and the daughters
of the men of the city come out to draw water

a good boy inserted in landscape

of light glint against a reflective surface light
makes us see the light down any dark
he saw
the tarrish canvas he could not admire such light

but the father was doing no evil was working
and the vision he produced his son's vision was
and the work of the father and the son was
necessary and the rope was strong
And the water was spent in the bottle, and she
cast the child under one of the shrubs

a radiation emitted, some anger, some
unguarded delight some danger

the fear of the visible

And Isaac's servants digged in the valley, and
found there a well of springing water
his mother's message her silence
a kind of accidental coding
Portent, Prodigy

We know this man's vision the dark against
which a streak of light agonized

48

in these paintings but watch   children pass
into witness they   schoolchildren pass
through the galleries talking among
themselves wishing for light, for watery light.

Did she mean when she said yes what he did
when he asked we do know better than
to watch the sun so bright it cannot be what
we see so loud the moon, meaning less yet

here is called morning glory, called
convolvulaceae, or asagao, Morning Face (in Japan)
and the sweet potato sweet (*Ipomoea batatas*),
commonly called yam in some united states

(I lived there and do no longer it was
called Home; called home is a name for death)
the sea and spring, and the random generation
of bloom and bad luck, we are known to ask

Is it True? the disquotational biconditional; or
a "one-time pad" an encryption algorithm
combines the message with the key as long as
the plaintext, used once like any life;

there are in cathedrals bell pulls, ropes
to grasp to climb into the weight of the bell
to spring upward a filament (of self)
lament if
a spidery line to, into the dark spire;

the last time I visited my brother before his death he ordered
us from his bed he directed us to set up the projector the tripoded
glass beaded screen and to dim the lights and he controlled the
projector and we watched light colored light and spoke a bit of
what light can mean how doubtful we were he dying me dying
too his face as a child mine in front of us light only glittering off
that screen a warm hum from the projector as the lenses and the
emulsion heated and gave off a metallic scent which was a hint
a word related to hunt but not exactly a search an opportunity

49

Do you know the invention of tools, how to?
You, Human, you made them yourself. It is how
you became immortal, making things.
It is a code you made yourself, a way to read

Museum item 94.09.171 (*mano*)

if I say the most interesting thing about the
item is the number inked onto its side
if I say this is what I first see in the photograph
if I say the item itself resembles the size
shape and color of a potato

this is not to deprecate but to pray
and add some measure to my own worth, word,

for the number calls to mind Shoah
for the potato calls to mind famine
for the photograph calls to mind light
writing and the act of seeing, artifact,

for the shape fits the hand
for the hand is sister to vision
for the hand formed the brain

for vision occurs in the lateral geniculate body
then the striate cortex

for I have a pen and I can make that kind of mark
and I must eat and I have a hand
and I have a past, dim, doomed, memorial.

"But the world is not a bottle from which
light escapes like smoke" wrote Roubaud
but in French but Rosmarie turned it to
the light of English which is all I know, I
know how the well was wet and dark and
the pipe casing was cracked and the boy

would not call out his fear but the boy
would be good and silent and would watch
feeling the rope against his ankles lowering
low into the erased earth where there would
be water soon and a well is a tool
only empty erasure and I did

I did throw stones down there some the size
of that mano one might have been a tool
some human made some dark
day we all know the streak of light like
or a spark against the steel.

TREATMENT OPTIONS

Inside, the palm and fingers,
remain young to mock the blotted
asters of the back of the hand

the young are much alike we
separate into selves;
the young know each other.

Reveron, after diagnosis,
made dolls for which he made
birdhouses and birds

the threshold is horizontal
the pillar vertical
and there a world intersects

I know such people, across
their palms lines deepen

you will catch them

staring, horrified, into it,
the cup of self before them
a universe engaged and silent;

or consider a hand
like a mirror is nothing in
itself, neither adds nor subtracts

from the self reflected.
He made dolls for which
he made beds and clothes

and books and groceries
and love of a sort, miniature
love and hats and gloves

with fingers. Breakable but

not divisible. Fingers removable
from the hand, the glove.

A rule of thumb, save
someone daily, self
included. Cheerfully.

(Armando Reveron, 1889-1954: "they only look. It is I
who speak. They look at me and listen to me")

THE CITIZEN AT THE DOOR

A body that could never rest
Since this ill Spirit it possest   (Marvell)

now is   present   "Do you
then was   past   love it"
soon   future   he said to
within which all comes clear   the image
                              which was
                              really only
to begin again the search meaning a shadow,
a solid metal heated   his own
                         shadow on
liquified splashed   the wall in
against a flat stone   front of him
or a surface of water,
makes a shape to read   sometimes
                         beside him
and it is a past, shining   as he walked
droplets of   (until corrosion begins)   slowly with
no (longer) liquid record   characteristic
     (molybdomancy)   gait: a shuffle

or to blow out the candles while   some call it
friends sing, singe on this burning   recognized
wax celebratory, celebate from which   by all as
                         if not
bees make babies, flowers turn   dangerous
into bees in   time   a sign of
The citizen at the door   discomforting
                         discourse
closes the door and the man moves   to come: most
on pursued by police since some call,   cross the street
                    avoid him
take offence or fright at his hand   to avoid him
a fist for knocking at doors and he   most cross
knocks at doors, the fist painted   and he does
white then when a door opens he opens   not notice

the fist fingers forward from his face   or if he
obscuring his eye to reveal   notices he
painted on his palm an eye, larger than   says nothing
life. Taken for observation he   who has little

is taken who has   future
done so little, a life little   a thin present
life. Odd how large a vision   and a past
how sensitive we are to the face   no more dense
the symmetries the scale   than the thin
   thickness of his own shadow sliding painfully across the
         concrete and brick of wall and street.

ADDRESS DIRECT

That cacophony of breath and blood you hear
is not code for any comfort it is blood
and air moving within you, you

Stimmen, stemming the tide of fluids
your little frightened faces inner only linger
then anger then it ends then this thinly

for my crimes I know
and my offense is before me always (Psalm 51:5)

stammer your salvation—
to say is to succumb, would be—who
cannot say—for the impediment

the course of conditionals bleeding
into themselves like internal injury
and yet the day declares a truce

with you, your friendship intact
your body at your bidding
a lithe loveliness still there and

fertile, furtive and funny.

COMPUTATIONAL ORIGAMI

All is surface. Her face, erased of age timely leaning
into an image imagined mirrors idly an afternoon ago, a ghostly
layer of herself a moment moving a surface a face a primordial
phenomenon of gentleness. It is cosmic, cosmetic to see so great
a comfort there : she opened her own wrists like you would an
envelope only with a sharper knife

: they're there, she said, Here, hear; let's not play games, let's play
things like music a note a note found: we shed as we pick up like
travellers who must carry everything in their arms and what we let fall
will be picked up by those behind. (Septimus, *Arcadia*, Tom Stoppard).
She, collector, folds cranes of paper; folds families of corvidae,
folds and folds.

Birds and geraniums bloom from her hands her agonies
folded and filed, fill cabinets. The lure of the pelargonium. Given
an arbitrary polygon, can you construct creases so that when you fold
on all the creases, all of the boundaries of the polygon lie along a single
straight line? (Robert Lang). She wants her paper flowers to grow,
she wants her paper cranes to fly; she throws a bird into the air like
a rock, a ball. The bird never lands. Effaced. She collects paper and
every cranny of her home fills furious shiny and hidden
a life aligned a face.

ANOMALIES OF WATER

Phase Anomalies

Water melts at a high temperature…liquid ice
inspires concern and delay, delights the ignorant
and the adept;

water boils at a temperature high enough to destroy
the world, this one, the one you're standing in

while its critical point involves the lesser gasses
their febrile machinations anguished in the night,

the night of stable crystals and amorphous mineral structures,
this night, the one you are traveling though, you who care,
careening;

the thermal conductivity of ice reduces with increasing pressure,
hence the waiting, the dissipation, and the dread,

the white hair of the waters combed, combined
with warm which vibrates longer than the cold.

Density Anomalies

At extremely low temperatures the density of ice
increases with heat up to seventy degrees Kelvin

but water shrinks as it melts and pressure reduces the
melting point, o ice o clarity; now

Ignis gnosis, to ignore is to ignite; the face centered cubic
engaged ignores crystalline structures

altering altering altering The walls are strong
and I am weak (John Berryman) the melting point

of water is over one hundred degrees higher
than suggested by extrapolation of the melting points

of the other group six A hydrides… *For water moves*
and flows with so very small a moving power
because it is made of small rolling shapes (Lucretius)

Material Anomalies

Water shrinks on melting, as do all who cry
Mineral child, miner, minor, mine

the salt and a kind of melting of the eyes
a tear a tear a terror   why name such waters

such times of evening, the light above
the darkness rising, the gray the blue the dreary:

a miller became poor then a Nixie appeared to him
and promised to make him wealthy if he promised

to give her what was being born in his house
at that moment a son a surprise promised alas

to this spirit of the water this fair fiend of water
D_2O and T_2O differ significantly from H_2O

deuterium tritium hydrogen two three one
the boy grown carelessly too close to the water

and the Nixie rose up and seized him and the story
lengthens there is a wife who saves him a flute

and a comb and a spinning wheel all in water all drowning
the flood the flood the flood the

Nixie tried to drown them but the wife
called the old woman who turned her into a toad

and him into a frog the flood separated them they
regained their human forms on land far
apart and forgetful

they became shepherds they met without knowing
each the other but he played a flute   she remembered

playing a flute to rescue him so she wept
and they wept water with and various salts
besides lysozyme,

the antimicrobial properties of tears have been explained
by their high concentration of lactoferrin, betalysin, and

secretory immunoglobulin A "Nixie" ultimately
from the same Indo-European base as Sanskrit *nij-*,

Greek, Old Irish *nigim* (Irish *nigh*), "to wash"

Thermodynamic Anomalies

the electron densities of the different isotopic forms
of liquid water have proved, so far, to be indistinguishable,

it is expected that the O-D bond length is shorter than that of O-H
due to its smaller asymmetric vibration and the smaller Bohr radius

of D relative to H. This gives rise to small differences in the size
and direction of the dipole moment between HDO and H_2O,

which further confuses any analysis of the structure of water
containing mixed hydrogen isotopes.

Water has higher specific heat capacity than ice or steam
Steam is invisible—it is not the fluffy stuff

it is the dangerous clarity coming out of the pipe,
the few inches of gas which then cools into droplets

He took me to his work inspecting the boilers
at the hospital, caves he guided me through he knew

water and knew the corrosives which hid in heat
and would eat metals back into the soil; Water

has an anomalously high heat and entropy
of vaporization and of sublimation.

Physical Anomalies

Water has oddly high viscosity yet unlike
the amber agony of honey engages light,
enthralling molecules colorless

paths into the ragged realms where
the rabbi and the rabbit flee the same flood

all flee the same flood; but no aquaeous solution
is ideal and as the temperature of water falls

viscosity increases and as density with pressure
increases, self-diffusion of water increases

and water can bounce because of its unusual
high surface tension, and bounce, *bunsen,*
is an old word water is a word

the Gibbs adsorption equation: a decreasing
surface tension corresponds to an enhanced ion

concentration at the interface contrary to expectations
based on Onsanger-Samaras theory...

the loneliness only grows deeper
the deeper the surface slides…

here and there a desert lies, and here
and there a survivor: (translated by Sylvia Beach:

*I add one further word to you, a question rather. Does water flow in
your country too? (I do not remember whether you have told me so)
and it gives chills too, if it is the real thing.* Henri Michaud)

What heat we feel we wear we weather
wilted selves learning to be
water and salt and little else, self.

POSSIBLE WORLD SEMANTICS

Scissored, like a little dance

A riddle; flowers in a field were once
women. One was allowed to dance
with her lover in his house at night.
She said: If you pick me
in the morning I could stay
with you forever. Question:
the flowers were identical;
how did he know which to cut?

I make a new mistake each time I tell
this story. It is an ancient telling, full
of the counted dead, the lovers.

These flowers in the field at night grow
wet with dew; the one in the house does not.
He cuts the dry one, or counts his choices.

Ataxia

Caused by a lesion in the cerebellum
for instance. See also posturography,
Romberg's sign, gait ataxia, locomotor
optic and sensory ataxias. Order
abounds at the shrine of St. Vitus at Ulm
attracting sad choreiform shakers;

how to tell the illness from the patient?

"They danced until three the next morning
when their shoes were danced to pieces and they stopped.
The princes rowed them back across the water."

Adaptive Optics

Stars move eyes follow. Or she put on
the dress of stars it glistened like the night
she danced with the king who slipped a ring
on her finger to hold her—to mark her
yet she escaped into the crowd then
back into the kitchen where she hid
her dress of stars glistening.

The stars appear to vibrate in the night
but it is the air which moves the light.
And yet the air moving is sound, if heard,
a song, so air dances with starlight.

Well, so walk away from the party
you are bored there is no one to dance with
the band the drink the dresses the need so necessary.

Tarantism

Possibility and necessity combine to yield a
Possible World economy. A proposition, p,
is a necessary truth if it is true in all possible worlds;
"Here" is an indexical: its meaning is indexed to
where the word is uttered. "Now" is an indexical:
indexed to the time the word "now" is spoken. The
actual world is the possible world that we inhabit.

Taranto is a possible world and an actual world,
or was, when it was believed the tarantula's bite
could cause pathological dancing until the poison
was danced out. Tarantella. A possible dance,
a necessary dance, indexed to then not now.

64

Early Onset

If it is a story it is a sad story my friend who was sad
moved into the light (California)

but I have stories of my own of oranges growing on
trees like money for every passing

stranger and of a child sleeping like cats in the sun
the story sleeps like cats in the sun

the sun shines mutely against the mouth the lips shape
themselves in sleep according to

a silence of happiness the forests of my childhood are
stories, songs silenced by

my own poor memory or is it illness the beginnings
going of going to forget is less

painful than we thought then a poverty of memory
a maimed mind there was always

jasmine and there were fierce birds guarding
the jasmine no but there was once

jasmine and always birds will come when I call
if I call.

from

The Difference between
Night and Day

(1978)

ENTROPY

Some of the evil of my tale
may have been inherent in our
circumstances.
        —T. E. Lawrence

I

Petals of poppy burn
a brilliant hole in landscape:
the land lies riddled with heat.
The murders our evening paper tells
are not those we each commit
under this stress of heat.
Among our flowers butterflies
tatter their flimsy lives. Pray
for the drowning city,
but for the city consumed by heat
listen to the scatter
of its dry seed.

2

The formidable memory of birds
brings them back by millions
each summer. For two days
the sky darkens beneath their wings,
their call is that faint language
a citizen barely recalls:
a thin, scattered remembrance
of an age of flight.

And we become a city of lizards
flat against the burning rocks
hanging shriveled sex in bundles
like garlic from the rafters,
an amulet against dangers.
We fear what comes with the cool
of evening, are terrified of sight.

3

And we fear such things as great success
or obvious failure. We know ourselves.
Each house in our town has a garden,
a wall, and a secret. We breed garish flowers
to tend with care. We are
small and all much alike.
In our city if you need a place to sleep
knock on any door. If it opens, the smell
of fear may drive you back into the street.

Let us consider that our fear is a large black bird—
this is hypothesis—and this bird's solemn
wing beat marks a cycle of months, perhaps years.
In our beds at night we breathe longer breaths
to keep time with our peculiar fate.
We go slowly through the day, we try to be part
of what we do not understand. I have kept
our secret but told you of our fear.

4

Wrapped in yourself speak
to us as a prophet should, fresh
from the desert. Tell us the story
of stones and small immortal snakes,
the story of long effulgent time.

5

On the first of July, 1961, Louis-Ferdinand Céline
spoke in our Municipal Auditorium. The speech
was called "Life Comes to You in the Morning."
I shall not be great in my own language, he said,
I am one who grows in translation.
There was much applause, and a clown show followed.

The speech lasted twelve hours. We heard
the purr of bees, the brittle crash of fountains,
voices in the distance rising and falling
like flocks of birds. We saw the spittle
dry on his lips. He spoke

one long single breath, and at the end
only I was left to hear.

I alone applauded, till my hands bled;
I threw the poppies to his feet;
I alone saw the clowns
perform unspeakable acts
upon each other.
later, the speaker and the clowns gone,
I watched the spiders
weave stars in the rafters.

6
A man drives his car in the desert.
He is alone. Our city lights the sky
in a small corner of his horizon.
Soon he will sleep, or die, and dream
of acres and acres of poppies
with butterflies skimming their surface
and a few magnificent spiders
drifting on threads,
riding the waves of heat.

MARTYRDOM: A LOVE POEM

Each of the dozen saints is bound
to his own stake like a prize tomato.
We know each death will bear
a flame red fruit.

When necessity lugs us into another year
do not be misled by calendars, a new year
begins with each tick, each time you
remember time is passing. And what a pet
you've made with a numbered dial
around time's neck, a leash
of pendulum to walk it once
around the block before sleep.
At night time gathers itself, a pack
of neighborhood dogs to knock over
your garbage cans, to gnaw discarded
secrets scattered for the neighbors to see
if they, bothered by the noise, will look
at small lives withering in the dew.

You and I owe nothing to sanctity,
find there no help, nothing dangerous
makes us what martyrs are—
we have visions of each other
in our sleep, we know the secrets,
we have touched. We love because
it grows late and the tomatoes
are ripening. A morning glory
climbs one stake, mingles with
green and pink-striped fruit: tomorrow
we will look at what's been done.

Certainly I would die for you:
that is the easy part, like falling
from grace or off a log.

TO BURY A HORSE IN TEXAS

Thirty years old, the only horse
we owned died on Christmas Eve:
my mother watched the feet flashing
in winter light trying to touch ground.
She cried. Father shot three times
did not know the spot but somewhere
between the eyes it
took the hint, gave up.

What do you do with a horse dead
for Christmas, the renderers closed
till New Year, flies catching the scent?
You and all your brothers dig
while the sun shines, you watch
its side where a last breath
gathers through the day.

The yellow earth opened beside it.
We dug close to drag it less far.
We covered it. For Christmas
that year I got boots and guns
to play at cowboy.

In the white night a horse floats in awful
phosphorescence. The mad child rides
brandishing silver guns with the message
in red on the barrels: Kill him for me,
                    I am so young.

from

White Monkeys

(1981)

THE MAGICIAN

From up my own sleeve I came
and chose my father,
a volunteer from the audience.
I told him to stand
there, in front
of the buzzing saw.
I grabbed him by his long
ears and pulled him
into the hat with me.
There in the silky dark
we slept.

I used to know lots of tricks.
Pick a card, any.
I memorized a card a week
for a year. I turned
rabbits into plowshares.
I escaped from every kind
of closure.

In the hat we slept together
dreaming each our games
of solitaire.
We awoke old;
forgetting everything
we bowed goodbye.
I last saw him walking away
trying to wipe his eyes
with a white handkerchief
that kept becoming a pigeon.

ECLIPSE

Recall the light
that moved under the bedroom door,
that sifted through the dust-mice caught
beneath the bed, then was gone.
It was your mother in the hall,
deep in the night—the sound of water
from the bathroom, the whine of plumbing
like the torturer's bride escaped
into the wall.

I could not turn
away from their flash when distant
visiting relatives took pictures:
I stared at the blue bulbs
they licked then stuck in steel
sockets. Afterward, the seared spot
still floating in my eye,
I would secretly peel the plastic
coating off—a safety device,
they told me, in case the glass globe
should explode.

My father held
the black, nearly opaque sheets for me
to protect my eyes, he said, but that
I would remember this eclipse forever.

The papers carried stories of two boys
gone blind from unprotected staring.
They should have had such a father
as mine, I said, but wondered
what it was like, that last moment
of sun, that ring of corrosive light
just at that moment beyond recall.

PLEASURES OF THE FLESH

I watch her in the morning look
at three birds brooding on a wire
like suicides on a ledge.
She knows its uselessness
how she would only spread wings
to save herself at the last moment.

Sadness is neither virtue nor vice
though it has caused music,
and flowers and pathetic smiles
to line the long highways of our state.

from

The Language Student
(1986)

THE CATS OF BALTHUS

We must bear witness to something.
At the Château de Chassy, near Autun,
Balthus Klossowski de Rola eats breakfast
under the green eyes of Mitsou, Angora.

In the painter's eye girls forever
sprawl like morning sun among the hassocks
and fainting-sofas. They drink tea
the color of sunrise and as bitter.

At the Château de Chassy the sun
tries hard to be nameless in spite
of the painter's eye and will
to tame it, drape it across the proper chair.

But he will not tame the cats,
and only pretends to name them
for the neighbors' sake. They drape
where they like, leave their marks

on the muslin, chew through the doilies
the shape of white suns; they leave
their film of hair thickening
on the furniture. They sprawl.

We would like to look at the girls
doomed to adolescence, to see them
through the wide windows he offers us
as if we, on the way home late,

the evening's carouse given way
to gray sunrise, were caught by the slight
movement of girls in the house; as if
we stand in the shrubbery to look

then notice ourselves noticed
by the cat, its green eye narrowing
as we both stare at the jungled coast.

SYLLOGISM

If every good boy deserves favor, and all cows eat grass,
then music, like milk, is made of sly croppings
of green blades glistening some mornings in dew
and desire, of the wish to be better and do more.

Nothing returns whole unless transformed.
The insinuant twitter of birds in the barn when the boy
does chores before school, these sounds return
when his drink is stronger, his love of life weaker
but better for being not duty but desire.

Sing something, solemn boy, and press your head deeply
into the flank of the cow while the music of milk
deepens in the bucket. All flesh is grass.

THE LANGUAGE STUDENT

A small, dark man, I'm often
mistaken for foreign.
Tourists greet me in Spanish;
a serious man in a suit
once whispered in Farsi
while watching my eyes.
As I boarded a plane
the pilot once said
Comment dit-on femme
en Anglais?

At home I often lie in bed
staring through the ceiling
with clasped hands behind my head.
Sometimes in winter I sit
before the heater and smoke
cigarettes in the dark:

but if I could learn the language
I could walk pebbled paths
beneath blooming trees
as a casual foreign elegance
wafts smoky through the air,
as ferocious women and tame dogs
ask me to follow them home.

from

The Erotic Light of Gardens

(1989)

SOMETHING TO SAY

So where is there but the body to live?
Many have searched. The young seem to like it,
slitting their wrists in joy then languishing
long afternoons in the melting heat.
Even you and I, in that city of damp and delicate
air, we too spent an afternoon or two of spending.

There is no place else to live, but we mustn't
say so. There is nothing left, after the mind goes
and the spirit reveals itself for its own
thin soup of despair; refuge and reconciliation
and the lingering doubt when the tendons strain
against the weight of the head, the tendency
of each part to go its own way, of the hands to shake
palmate and practical, the toes to catch on hosiery
while teeth wear themselves to powder.

There are children, of course, who watch the wind
one afternoon, the leaves turning graceful
in some handy tree. Watch the face of some
child laughing under there, and think
of your mother back home, your father dead,
all your brothers busy with their lives, no one
thinking about what the child must do with a body
wrapped around him like blankets from firemen
after disaster some winter night:

it's why we invented language. The gallop
of the tongue across sharp teeth, the exotic
dance in there of flesh and bone and breath.
There's nothing like talking to take it all away,
all the body's ailments, its little pains
and purple bruises, its criminal tendencies.
Words filter from the skin, and sweat pours
defensively down from the brow and we eat our bread,
and all this time we thought it was sex

that saved us, we thought we were thrown out
for pleasure, and really, all along,
pain was its own reward.

HARVARD CLASSICS 16,
THE THOUSAND AND ONE NIGHTS

1

The lives of former generations are a lesson to posterity.
The lives of the dead Serve none of their own purposes.
That a man may review the remarkable events which have happened,
that someone learn something and be admonished, or at least amazed,
consider the history of people of preceding ages
and be restrained:

As if the telling of tales could save lives and virginity
and teach that nobility lies in complexity,
since it was to Complexity that Shahrazad prayed
while her sister Dunyzad served only the gods
Complication and Confusion.

The color of flesh is always shocking;
the veil slipped through no one's fault
aside to reveal the searing light of skin
or the horrifying glimpse in the mirror after your bath
and the dreadful fit of that skin or,
perhaps for the lucky, the sudden lust.

So a woman lay in his bed and told stories all night
which is the same as the astronomer in his celibacy
asking the only questions worth asking,
those with no end of answers,
or at least none before sunrise.

2

What lacks passion lasts. In my own childhood
I told myself stories long into the night;
later they became erotic, and full of other
heroics than violence. I climbed the trees
whose scent and fallen needles and touch
of scaling bark could take the skin off.
Sometimes a seed fell, a brown wing broken

from among the sharp edges of the cone
(curious geometry, those fruit) twisting
in sunlight frightening as bad dreams.

I played soldier among the trees
killing quite adroitly quaint masses
of enemy—plenty to choose in the fifties,
Germans, Japanese, Koreans, the faint
remaining trace of Indians.
The lives of former generations
are a lesson to posterity.

But war well made by boys becomes
a further innocence, a pastoral procession
from a distance, like sheep grazing
beneath the cedars of a far hill,
a simple oriental pleasure like Lebanon,
and women will tell stories in the night
without end; or else I slept through it all,
perhaps lived better than I knew or loved.

3
So the child volunteered her flesh
and life to save, perhaps, the virgins
of the tribe, she the daughter of the Vizier's
complicity—and was he evil? or the king
himself a moral monster? The books don't say.
Only that he killed them, out of fear
of repetition, his sultry modern mania
for the original, for verse without reverse.

There followed a thousand further versions.
There followed the consideration of histories
of preceding ages, and the contemplation
of the woman's flesh, the veil and flimsy fabric,
that he might be constrained
spread out as he was on this earth like a bed.

LIFE RAFT

Once there was a difference
between pain and desire. The world
was not safe: ships sank, fathers
sacrificed sons to gods, and mothers
abandoned whole households, children
trussed and tossed into closets
dark as the undiscovered psyche.

And there were dangerous men who believed
that art, say, "Raft of the Medusa,"
was compensation for events, say,
the falling of hungry men upon
the flesh of the dead on
that famously fragile craft.

The world's necessary nourishment
will be provided: there are needs
greater than accuracy. Géricault
gathered heads from the guillotines
for study; little piles all over
the studio floor. And had brought
to him limbs from the hospitals
of Paris, amputations for study,
little piles of flesh:

there are several ways to suffer,
not all of which are art.
As his usual practice meant sketching
until the paper darkened like evening
wracked with lines, he would trace
the best parts onto fresh paper
and go again—hundreds of versions
piggybacked of some twisted leg or two.

True, he was once famous for horses,
lively and lithe and vegetarian.
And at his own end, hospitalized,

93

he had no model but his own hand
to draw—how like the man of passion,
this recourse to one's own hollow palm,
whatever one's art or eros.

Nevertheless, after hundreds of studies
leading to the final painting, none
of those cannibal themes remained;
but what does any art consume
if not its own and maker's flesh?

THE PRIVATE TOUR: CIRCLE 7, ROUND 3

What boy doesn't, once, admire his father?
There was nothing to be known he didn't know,
that day, about water. I entered behind him
the great electrical caverns where cascades like
the tropics fell cleanly to cool air
for operating rooms; I crawled with him through
boilers down, bulging with rust and power.

He taught me to titrate, and to pronounce
fine-grained words, and to think full phrases
like parts-per-million, like Erlenmeyer flask.

When he dies he divides the world precisely
as any chemist can. Having ridden the beast
he tells his child, I will ride between you
and the tail, lest you be poisoned by it.

from

Massacre of the Innocents
(1995)

WHEN CULTURE WAS POPULAR

1

The flamingo would turn in the wind on one leg.
And a cat. A lawn. An afternoon. The snail
had a bad reputation but climbed forever
the razor's edge to the moon leaving only
a mucous memory. This was America.
This is political. The world as rock with
a liquid center, bonbon of stone with
a powdery organic skin.

2

I thought of the weight of the silly planet
as last night another city burned, pity
its loss, TV the culprit. Watched men on the
moon, did that man dream on the moon?
The angel I know best has a small face
and large hands and no power but that
of speech. He is tired but immortal.
Laplace would argue that if both position
and momentum of a particle were fully known
at a discrete moment and all forces acting
upon the particle fully known, then
the particle's motion is fully determined
for all future time. Time future all. For
determined fully is motion. All interesting
novels are about a man who murders
(a foreigner after the funeral of) his mother.
The moon has a solid center. It is foreign.
It is female like a pink angel on the lawn.

3

Since revolutions go in circles we suggest
a fine delicacy, a step in a straight line,
a legacy: the maid saw things would straighten
your hair, Mister; would make your sister
weep. The maid has things to do, but if
you spoke Spanish you could ask her while

the cars go fast on the interstate. The trains
don't stop for people, and trees live in pots;
you can turn them to get the best light.

History was her best subject and she voted
every chance she got. She tried to do it
right. She used to be your mother. Look
at the terrific birds, the shining feathers
made into banners for the exhibit, remember
the Aztecs could turn a million hummers
into one king's hat. Nice nature. Close
to the land, that's how to live. Put
yourself in their place, a glorious casualty
wandering home at evening the angle of sun-
light reddish and warm. The fall not yet
threatening, just a rumble in the distance
while a glamorous casualty waits at the bus stop
for her friend, a future to take home.
Here is history, how it sounds: what
do I love? Remind me.

4
We used to listen to the muttering
of Popeye defeating the lesser races,
vegetarian Popeye armed with unrequited
love for a slender woman. I like secret
agents of my own animation, me
about to be invented lying awake
imagining that the dawn waits patienter
than lovers. I have always known the world
is full of hunger and anger and despair
a form of which is loneliness:
some is my fault, some my reward. Small
wonder there is a city named La Paz
where the beautiful step-daughter
attracted the old man's attention,
the old man who spit on his hand
then with the other hand touched
her hair; who knew? Bolivia
exports tin and bauxite and keeps

the beautiful names (Sugar and Peace
in a manner of speaking) for capitals.
Wicked step-parents learn to live
in penumbrae of beautiful daughters,
serpents in the gardens. So lie
in bed and rehearse, reverse
the regulation of the arable, all
the patterns spinning like an old
man of La Paz returning in dream
spitting on that hand as if to
grip the plow.

(Or maybe you preferred Krazy Kat and
the accurate artillery of love, mouse-
thrown bricks crashing. Isn't it just
like opera, couldn't you just die
waiting and waiting for Spiderman
to pendulum past the window telling
good jokes killing bad men. Couldn't
you live that way?)

5
Comic books, Japan, Anything, Stars
to talk about, loneliness works this way:
the empty seat next to you on the bus
as audience, the city passing quickly
and the weather never alters. Text
and illustration:

Wonder Woman flew an invisible airplane
dotted lines emblem of its shape memory
a poem of the mind's eye seeing.
With a golden rope she evoked
involuntary truth from trussed
enemies. A golden age. Trust

Japanese men in small suits riding
trains at hundreds of miles per hour
gathering cleanly to talk business and love.

Here is the hard one: openness like the sound
when you press your ears closed not like
an ocean at all. The roar of blood, home
again where the house echoes. Something
breaks two blocks away and the glistering
sound stays forever, its own memory.

It would be good to teach a child the names
of each: Beehive, M44, Praesepe, any chart
would do: the Chinese made the Milky Way
a barrier between lovers, self control not
their virtue, the lovers. If a star
falls, is there a sound.

6
"Dear _____, I walk around
these mountains, monstrous things full
of rock, basalt bands ribboning them.
the birds are black billed magpies
each with a history and insect digesting.
The wind rising whirls itself
around corners of this protruding world.
I walk around these mountains full
of horizons slipped onto their ragged
edges, the end of landscape becoming
a picture like a pretty melody, a girl.
The birds are black with long tails
and streaks of white. Like ghosts
they fly like angels. Against
the wind the birds are beaten
back as memory fills them with despair.
Sincerely, _____."

7
Dreaming on the moon a man dreamed on
the moon he said: "I dreamed I found footprints
not ours over a hill..." when in his little mobile
home his flying turtle-shell his pup tent
his boy scout house he slept;

a child could not nurse there no mother's
child could nurse in that moon night that light
you need the weight of atmosphere the air of earth
conspires to spill a little milk into the mouths
of babies. Lover please forgive my life, come

back and try again to talk to me. The light
is so sweet and the birds sing and everything.
We have air and summer night and insects
hover uncrushed in its weight their short lives.

GENIUS ENGINE

Slide rules in belted leather cases
log-log rules sliding sexual
in the hand with lines of fine print
graven on bamboo white plastic coated
hand-made heroism in those days of
engineers into the night calculating
approximately. Neighboring numbers
blended as the eyes tired. How words
work is, you pay attention elsewhere
until you remember you said yes to
something that worked, it made a life.
But in the night my brother cries pillows-
ful of confusion seeing visions coined
by an ancient emperor to keep awake.
Over and over while needs grow thick
in the duckpond our work was to make
the world work with days of analog
computing, long wooden blades in our
hands while we watched the rippled
race racing across the surface during
the dark of evening at the point where
wind wiped quick breath on the mirror
held to mouth in the movies.
We were all Americans, we boys were all
first among equals. There was a time
I knew something, a realism the conspiracy.
I wept bright coins and paid my way.

A TREE FULL OF FISH

(Nine Dreams of a Girl)

Sleep

    is a place where you can dive as if into water but not
drown. She knew that. It was where she felt safe.
Sometimes she thought she was followed but
she was good at losing them,
at hiding behind corners until the feeling passed.

Her mother would read to her at night
to make her dream. The parent reads what the parent wants
the girl to dream. So she would listen for a time
but soon would recall her own dreams,
then would pretend she was asleep as a way to begin
and then her mother would give up and to herself
finish reading the story silently in the dark as
large-mouthed bass prowled the silt-darkened rivers
outside her windows. The flame-stitched pillows
on the couch coolly burn. She would jump
from an imagined rock and the splash
would follow her down and the bubbles would glide
with her to the bottom where the light shone
dimly, where she heard Christmas carols in the distance.
Dangerous mothers spent days shopping for patterns,
turning the large stiff pages of catalogues, turning
slow faces to the metal cabinets aligned endlessly;
Mothers would slide open the heavy drawers to find
the right red fish for Halloween or a sad little elf
for Christmas. This was the first dream.

Another Dream Was during

    the time of the world's tallest mountain, the light coming down
from the North as drawn in all the relief maps, the imaginary North the
imaginary light as a clean moment. She climbed steadily without pause

and heard vaguely from below the sound of her mother's lost voice on
and on telling her some story about some child who wandered the woods
alone until wolves or grandmothers ate her. It would be odd to live inside
an animal or a grandmother or a whale, like a bubble; the clean mountain
with the light coming straight from the North is better

it is better not to drown than to marry.

The Third Dream Recurrent

as fever diminished the world in the eyes of the child,
the torment delivered whole and clean to her tiny pathos.
Listen, she said to herself, you are a child,
this all-night arrogance is beyond you; play a little,
give yourself some credit. She was so small
and full of the larger virtues, like a saint
ready for martyrdom as any pear ripened.

Christmas like a wave on a pond the pebble thrown infinitely
the little waves wash at the toes of all the children sleeping
around the world awaiting some silent visitation, some creature
coming to punish or to praise;

the holidays are full of this kind of wisdom
like Jerusalem, so full of fate
and long anger. To be a child who dreams is to walk in danger.
She will wake now, she is so tired.

War Is this Dream To a Child

whose father was there, whose father in the night fights the
television enemy, whose father remembers and sleeps two rooms
down the hall and sleeps with a light burning, never never in total
dark horror.

What child can live like this, with a father who was there and,
proud of his wounds, wounds all children in the neighborhood
and sleeps only with a light.

Slowly as the horses of the night she rode them down the hall
to her father's door, the light under the door, the sound of her
father's sleeping soft as something gigantic back there sleeping
sleeping;

go to him, someone said nearby, he needs you. So in her little
red costume the only daughter dances down the hall to listen to
the story of the war and the French farmhouse where the farmer's
daughter had a clean bed and no past and no future like any every
child.

The Fifth Christmas Dream

      of such a child was simple who said her little prayers
now I lay me down to sleep now I play the clown
too deep now my day will drown in sleep allow
the play to ground to creep living this way
the dangerous sisterhood of dream was full of divorce

diving straight arrowish into the center of the target of ripples
already there she became particle and wave in a complex of inter-
ference patterns zebra-like on the wall as the story her miniature
mother read to her sharpened to a point and the laughter turned
rhetorical burst:

she dreamed that kind of world this time, yes.

The Still, Still Life

The map she learned to follow was the back of her hand, the
islands of melanin, the throbbing veins draining to the wrist, the
months and years yielding:

there are those moments when she cannot speak to the world.
The dream continues into all those eels, els and twists,
letters. Nothing moves or nothing is ever still, either.
Lemons on a plate, light—you've seen the same yourself,
it's your life still

still her life after childhood stood there as in a closet or under
the bed. Anyone can have ambitions: the ambition to wake up, to
turn that corner uncaught, to leave the forest, etc. But it is never
enough since you have to sleep sometime, no matter how success-
ful your life otherwise. Think of Edison inventing the light bulb
then climbing onto the lab table for five minutes of sleep. The tree
twinkled behind the teacher as the teacher taught that story, as the
tale of hard work and practicality unfolded under the haunted look
of the angel atop the indoor tree, the tree dying the light bulbs
winking like an old man's leer in the parking lot (Christmas
ornaments, glass bubbles, fragile).

The Dream of the Inconsolable Desert

Sunday school and parochial discipline gave us stories of water
from stones and stone-shaped bread and yet no sense of desert as
tangible came into those upper rooms where the ecclesiastical
present presided over the historical past. The desert still holds
this attraction: as a place for the expiation of ancient guilt, fossil
guilt, there are no wells in the distance, no academic camel drivers.

At recess a game of soap bubbles. See the child
blowing her own soul through the eye of a needle—
it extrudes into the other side gleaming, sound
a perfection in three dimensions which attracts rainbows
but contains nothing more than the used, moist breath
of the child, the depleted oxygen and indifferent nitrogen
rejected by her tiny lungs.

"Writing is the childhood of the void, an exorcism of letters,
of words" —Edmond Jabès

Imagine the child diving into her own reflection—say
an extraordinarily smooth surface, say a lake of mercury
and the faces meet then disappear into each other,
dissolve, then the body parts collide, collapse
into themselves, their opposites—left hand
into right neither knowing for lack of leisure
what the other becomes;

say this smooth perfection continues, a snake
descending a limb, a lizard's tail following itself
into a crack in a rock—until the soft disappearance
of the tiny half-moon of the tip of the big toe
into light.

Among the little landmarks of a life, the hills
of desire see themselves mountains.

This is her dream gently waving like a flag across
every surface.

Dreams

analysis of. *See* dream interpretation, anxiety type,
of children, "day's residues" in, (Anna) Freud's,
Freud's lectures on, Freud's papers on, (William)
James on, Jung *vs.* Freud on, Pötzl on, prophetic,
recurrent, and telepathy, theories of, before Freud,
traumatic, as wish fulfillment, dreams, Freud's:
botanical monograph, cocaine in, Count Thun,
erotic, interpreted; in *Interpretation of Dreams*, by
Jung, of Irma's injection. *See* Irma's Injection dream,
about "Jewish question" (1898), about his mother,
"*Non vixit*," at Padua beer garden, his reluctance to
complete interpretation of, in his self-analysis, in
World War I,   —index to *Freud*, Peter Gay

The boys in the back of the room planning to be geniuses
examine the fascinating backs of their own hands.

A Three-Quarters Life-

sized Santa glows across her front lawn shining sanctity and
generosity into her bed across her sleeping face welling tears in the
year's eye. Seasonal greetings multicolored stream through the
mail. The visionary daughter of the household dreams triumphant.
All the questions of childhood tremble in the face of bedtime

reading then recoil against the necessary darkness of her closet
in spite of pink cashmere and the tiniest china dogs ranged
in rows formidable as the infantry of Napoleon. closet dramas
enact themselves through the night, a farce of doors opening and
closing escaping psyches and entrapped satisfactions.

To someone's daughter this happens in winter while awaiting a
new chance, a new year, a new number. Her mother wraps the
daughter's favorite ornament in the same white tissue each year, a
green glass fish, thought to dream, said to sleep.

from

Wake

(1999)

THE RUINED WORLD

(Its Glory)

It makes a music anyway
it is filled with beige plants and charcoal birds
it lingers
sunsets continue, chronic circling
rain will always fall
music breaks its heart
the barren seeds feed the birds
something moves
the light of a sun insinuates
puddles gather into lakes
sounds mingle into new chords
toothed edges of dry leaves cut
it cannot be stopped
it varies inversely with the square of the distance
its lakes reflect, on calm days
it makes its noises
its despised birds fly
it continues its turnings
the light is general and various
the noise of waves in the stormy nights
the sound of anything is a cleverness

but it remains a world. A place of consequence, of sequence. I pick
up scraps of paper and smooth them, pushing with both hands flat
against my thigh. The papers are various. I carry a tool for poking
in debris. I live this way.

The ruined world is mainly gray but the occasional flash, like the
epauletted blackbird you remember, is all the sweeter now for its
rarity. The air has its taste and its grit. The water is always brown.

The boatmen continue to love the world. The random riches, the fish.

Across the largest lakes the tinny bells still call for the faithful, beg
for forgiveness and a return to the fold. It is only the wind moving
among the ruins.

Nothing has changed.

Like many a voice of one delight,
    The winds, the birds, the ocean floods,
        The City's voice itself, is soft like Solitude's.

"Stanzas Written
in Dejection, Near
Naples" —Shelley

(Overheard)

Never trust the words. I do not
like the noise I make. It's all
I have, the noise I make, the trust. To make the words

a human failing. Noble silence is dead. Out of the depths
I cry unto thee o lord, lord hear my voice

fade softly into the hard discussion
who wouldn't like to know
this kind of consolation

word

…there is a group of words which etymologists are inclined to
treat as being all forms of the word which in O. Eng. is *sund*,
meaning "swimming." These words are (1) the swim-bladder of a
fish; (2) a narrow stretch of water between an inland sea and the
ocean, or between an island and the mainland, &c., cf. SOUND, THE,
below; (3) to test or measure the depth of anything, particularly the
depth of water in lakes or seas…in these senses has frequently been
referred to Lat. *Sub unda*, under the water; and Fr. *Sombre*, gloomy,
possibly from *sub umbra*, beneath the shade, is given as a parallel.
    —"Sound," *Encyclopaedia Britannica*, eleventh edition

not threatening
to hear while
casually under sun
it sounds like

rain and shimmering
small secret life
say some

story circling its way some
where the words wind
into tight knots stop then start
over
she heard a sound

as an infant she made faint noises, was called Good Girl
later she listened to her little records
on her boxy machine, which made her happy
a girl should be happy it is a world of sunlight
and the darkness behind the door is not her fault
the sunlight is made of those particles that penetrate the ether
shadows are an absence yes but make
the same sound as light
she plays in the sunlight she plays in the sunlight
"…as we were walking along
introduced me without warning to his habit

of suddenly quietly singing" —John Cage
A man at a public telephone in an airport
turns to the window to appear to be observing the landscape

("Using the term 'note' for a sound produced by a periodic
disturbance, there is no doubt that a well trained ear can resolve
a note into pure tones of frequencies equal to those of the
fundamental and its harmonics" —*Encyclopaedia Britannica*)

he cries a sound or two escapes he wears a dark suit
he carries a briefcase as he turns I pretend I am reading
I watch him leave I never see him again

How did he become who he is why does he
suffer

Kant: How can I know? What ought I to do? What may I hope?

to break the heart

thee o lord, lord hear my voice

My talkative friend bought a bicycle in his old age;
an interesting angularity, knees and elbows,   (S. Beckett)
walking stick attached to the handlebars for when he stopped.

All about bicycles he told, and about
the suicide, how hard it must have been
in that last moment to keep his aim for the tree;   (G. Oppen)
the one about the policeman during the war, in
Holland, who hummed constantly, they heard him coming, and his
        enemy the artist of contraband,   (S. Lenz)
how you could see a cyclist trying to escape for miles across
        that flat land;
and how the sounds of warning would carry,
and the whistling of the policeman, and the storms.

Boys say to fathers many words they have forgotten.

My father, too, knew words for things, the chemical compositions,
formulas that applied to the normal family. There was a terrible
dark form in the bottom of our bathtub, a vague shape rising
through the vitreous surface where he spilled hydrochloric acid.
He knew secrets of the soul, I am sure he did. He must have been
a man of passions, he would have told me if he could.

My friends all say there is much to talk about.
There is a sound to make that means happiness,
and there is a noise to accompany tears.

When Elizabeth Bishop wrote that the beach hissed like fat, what
did she damage? Not the future, which also hisses like fat. She said
the little birds skittered along the edge of the foam, that the
particles of sand when wetted by the seawater reassemble into a
denser surface and a sound results, a continuous sigh of the beach
itself, not the ocean. Oh the ocean has been known to speak for
centuries, such a claim is commonplace. And sand is a famous
symbol, to do with time. There is nothing more to be said.

On every continent even this very night
there are children crying, telling you of their guilt.
And there are chickens climbing into their roosts

muttering to themselves, beginning to nod
even as their lovely hard feet fasten tightly,
a special tendon doing the work all night.
And all the creatures of the world sigh
into their little futures, and close their eyes
and breathe for nothing but their need, quiet.

(Among Trees)

Among the laurus nobilis
conspiring molecules
quiver in light

fir or feathered
a tangle of tangent
the glitters radiant

pine and parameters
quercus virginiana
festooned

tillandsia usneoides
epiphytic bromeliads
bay

growing in my mother's yard also
laurel
hemlock

the light this way
green as if
it were one

thing
green as gravity
growing

Imaginably twisting groundward
and rot and riddling a massiveness of organization
organic, roots: mirrored by limbs and twirling loose
in air movement and marauding photons glancing

as if it were possible. Nothing more, as if from the bible
the love of trees something vastly and evil. Engorged.

The way to prophecy is to keep secrets.

We could speak of birds, or of air. Ether.

A hint is powerful. The way to god is ambiguity. A path
to his house, his hovel, his shelter under the trees.

A family among the trees begins to die, the generation
having gathered, all uncles and aunts to the world, the pace
of their aging not hurried but they die and gather a smaller
group each time around the gathering graves. Soon under
a liveoak one alone will wipe his brow and turn away.

"How tender the green tip before the leaf grows."
                                    —Robert Duncan

The enormous deciduous climb the gradual plain
the effect the geology of it all gone
there is a glitter beneath the wires the wind
plucks them a tone emerges the shatter
beneath and like longing turned crystalline
light light light

If the clouds be full of rain, they empty *themselves* upon the earth:
and if the tree fall toward the south, or toward the north, in the
place where the tree falleth, there it shall be. Eccles. II: 3.

A fill of forests and the story fills
us with regret and sweetness. We love
one another. The trees are ancient
and the story is long but no one tires
listening and great libraries flutter
from each limb and there is more to read
than ever can be told and more time
from the shade of the tree saunters

in front of the following sun
and still the story lingers.

(Preface)

A darkening delivers us
a children's game or simply
human shaped and sharp
a cowboy or some ethnic profile
toy soldier
formulas for anything and crowds
starlings change
shape forming and reforming against sunset

(into brightness in the dark
by the flame of his match he
felt the warmth of her hand on his
dissolve into the night the dark
he never saw such a face such
a woman smoke in the street walking)

there is your pattern of flourish
in this forest around the river
where Hansel wandered and Gretel
a flourish of blossom in the spring of fruit in the autumn
sadly slender humans descend their own nervous systems
eye to brain to spine
men do this and boys they look

(The amateur beekeeper should never work among his bees
without a veil, for stings about the face are particularly painful
and embarrassing.
              —*Beekeeping for Profit*, Randolph)

they look at
mingling with air, wave, waving there
awe and careless
through crowds of flesh the boys
look and burning with will they sell
buy and belong

(..it is characteristic of more refined humanity to respect "the
mask" and not to indulge in psychology and curiosity in the wrong
place.
　　　　　　—"What is Noble?" Nietzsche)

Lovely and true they are
to the ways of flesh, flash and awe

and teeth and lips and eyelids and lashes
jumbled flesh earlobes the tiny maze they dangle from
and the bones beneath to shape
a thing to gaze upon

he kept his most accurate
mirror in his own room well protected a little frightening

it is a game or toy a life is. I was happy
and you were beautiful and we danced like the movies
someone did. Those were the days.

And here Aeneas saw the son of Priam,
Deiphobus, all of his body mangled,
his face torn savagely, his face and both　　　　Aeneid 6, 651-655
his hands, his ears lopped off his ravaged temples,
his nostrils slashed by a disgraceful wound.

I would amazed listen
to the radio on the river the captains of ships conversing
the mates and enginemen the crackling
of two-way radio the rhythmic noise
and unamazed my uncle's sullen face hearing
his eyes closed his hand taking a shorthand
his understanding complete. I continued my games
hiding among the ship's stores and commerce
crates and gear to sell to passing mariners.
It seemed a game, this kind of life, of making a living
making believe, believing. This he could do
like child's play, his face behind his hand, hearing.

from the poem ESSAY

"When the small boats began gathering in the evening
to take us back after work, we would begin to stand
and get our backs accustomed to it, for we had mainly
stooped for the full ten hours, except
the little time they gave for lunch. Some would
stumble into the boats like drunkards, some
would step so carefully as if into
church, noses pointed forward. Some would be
sick on the trip back home, leaning
over the gunwales and drawing up the fish which
would gather on the greasy surface as the sun set
and the stars began to burn through the little light.
No one noticed this but me, all being too tired.
I don't know why I watched this way.
I needed to know something and found the world
a good enough subject."

A THEORY OF FANTASY

The boy his hand the size of the bird
Brilliant into the window pane the bird
The same heartbeat beat at the boy's
Wrist the folded wings. The bird revived
To stare at the view the aspens the
Mountains beyond. The bird flew and
I said You saved him. This art
Of lying we found alluring.
Boy and father staring at the aspens the
Mountains beyond.

We looked up the name of the bird studied the colors
And ranges. He tried to read the Latin like
A summer language. He failed.
As if evil were useful
He continued to dwell in that body not
Diseased merely doomed. And play to the world. Snow
Lay under the limbs of trees. The leopard lay with the lamb.
Contingencies threatened. He read himself
To sleep he dreamed spotted animals slink
Brain sex and muscle under pelt. Snow
Gathered by night by morning the world wore
Its white brain through which some crocus
Might break small and bright a language.

A LITTLE OVID LATE IN THE DAY

It is late in the day
to outlive the words:
tales of incest, corruption,
any big, mythic vice
against the color of sun,
the sweetness of the time of day—
I know the story,
it is the light I care about.
The book falls from my hands
and I know all the stories,
I know better than that.
They glitter in the grass.
This is fun in the summer,
the sun descending onto my back,
the weight of eight light-minutes
warm there against skin.
Someone will read aloud to me
when I have forgotten the words,
the look they make against the page,
the kind of stain it is against the paper.

SOMEONE WHISPERS BELOW IN THE GARDEN

Jemand flüstert drunten im Garten; jemand hat diesen schwarzen Himmel verlassen.
                              —*"Unterwegs,"* Georg Trakl

…someone has left this black heaven, someone
has forgotten…look how otherwise everyone is, how
easy it is to be happy.

This is an age when each room could be filled
with poems and music, every taxi arrive on time

I can buy three pears any morning, red ones
and green and gray and some with blue specks
like birds' eggs and some a sort of yellow
that used to be the color of Vienna

and nothing makes anyone happier than cats

and with my pears a bag of sunflower seed
to scatter and draw the birds within reach

and every window can be opened and every
sun can shine on someone or something
and the roads are clean and the trees end

but blue in the evening the rage rings
among the little trees in the toy forest,
the feral creatures tremble and wait for me
to offer my guidance, to spread
my arms and welcome them back
oh happy afternoon oh tiny grandeur.

LIVERY OF SEISIN

the delivery of property into the corporal possession of a person; in the case of a house, by giving him the ring, latch, or key of the door; in the case of land, by delivering him a twig, a piece of turf, or the like. —OED

Of touch, the annoyance
That if I touch you you
Touch me—the affront it is and

Its reciprocal nature and it is
The basis of the lighter
Perversions, frottage, for instance, which is

The secret joy of public
Touching it is, on a bus
To transport to touch the whole self

There is no stopping
It, if (there is no defense)
I touch you you touch me

If I touch (if not you)
The glamour of the stars
The stars famously beyond reach

That such light touches
The eyes the retina parts of the skin
The inevitable body (where we live no matter)

And too
The warm the sun striking out
But the stars softly at night (impossibly by day)

That we touch the stars
And that any light-
Emitting body (heat, any radiation)

Is infinite in size or will be
Caressing the universe
At a hundred eighty-six thousand

Miles per second
O love o sacred. To change
(To hold the house in your hand) the subject

To expand infinitely to the end
Too terrible to speak upon
Each man's life is but a breath (Psalm 39)

A touching most intimate,
The breath a column still attached
To the warm wet lung every leering man knows

What he's doing dreary
Perpendicular sounds/airs flying past
Touch extensive touch of someone's tongue

Expensive
O do talk less give us
Room, give us air dry and drifting

Flowers inventing
Themselves on the tips
Of trees reach out Nature reaches

Trees reach out like
Stars light their touch
And candor, all their own.

WAKE

Wast ever in court, shepherd? No, truly.
Then thou art damned

what can you do with a boy who wants the world beautiful who
would kill to make it so you must be careful with him yes kiss him
make him well notice the rain redeeming itself on your roof the
proof theological there the ambiguous there is a last rose in that
garden this fall dreary among the welter of leaves the arrogance
wearying talk me into it he said threatening love each the other but
we are no longer ancient in a narrow bed and we know some thing
or two—, compared to pain everyone knows pain but we were
young together going to the park with wine then the rain drove us
home where we opened our bottle and across the roofs of New
Orleans we watched the gray rain fall pretend we knew a hunger
for weather dismal that afternoon and dreary and gray the passing
and it is a coming into one's own entering even the language like
elephants into Italy no alp too high all trumpet and splash (the
flame of the match becomes the flame of the candle (or the split
amoeba becomes only itself forever) even if the match lies dead on
the carpet or *Bungalow* and *Bengali* as words curious to the English
ear confused but then Herodotus spoke of the aptness of belief
ears less than eyes the body being full of fun and mystery—
Mimosa was one of my favorites the word the tree left a mess after
rain on the sidewalk as of writing grapheme delicate pink soon
decayed to ink I read that in a book—I looked up from a book me
reading in the mountains toward the double rainbow one of many
in these mountains during this summer and there is no rainbow
only in the reader's mind the eye's trick mythic as any mirroring ear
is heir to—that place below the throat that delicate indentation
beloved by the hero of the novel of his beloved's body when it
mattered matter and the body the coming into one's own) "Safe
with my lynxes, feeding grapes to my leopards," Pound wrote the
man wrote early in a long dangerous career careening path (the
French for *quarry* as in hunt or stone) translation is hard
(crossroad career *carrière*) the French for anything in his small
memory of Mom and you'd think he'd grow up by now a life " And I

127

worship I have seen what I have seen" he knew so much and hated
so many he was sad as all get out at the end he ended that way
famous the cantos "And the frogs singing against the fauns in the
half-light. And…" So I was only eight years old and the night
before the trip I was saddened knowing now the trip was upon me
it was soon to be over and this excess of anticipation ruled my
remaining life the next night on the barge I smelled the lettuce,
bananas hung from the rafters near my sleeping- cabin and the
water below me indifferently brown crawled across to the Gulf to
an ocean and the water below me crawled across the mud and the
dead man and the detritus of where we lived in time of where I
spent that summer anticipating the dismal ending the return to
land and frogs singing I would remember forever the lights on the
river and the indifferent curl of wake as the great ships passed our
grocery barge where we would sell to sailors food and they would
sometimes tell us stories and they loved to tell us stories and at
night the smell of lettuce and bananas became stories to sell and in
the dark the ships' bells would hover and all of this in America
even though sailors were Greek and Russian and full of all anger
the river full of America swirling dangerous and brown full of wake
but day doth daily draw my sorrows longer And night doth nightly
make grief's strength seem stronger he said when it was necessary
he looked further into the night and turned beyond that last corner
turned tightly inward as the owls called as owls will to some
relative or against the random darkness, which is never perfect and
anyway is filled with the scratching of little feet clawed and clever
of endangered rodents still the man and woman turn toward each
other in the night who can ever forget such a moment such random
moments that make a couple of lives pathetic "Mr Pitt said that wd
/ surprise people here for that wars never interrupted the interest
of DEBTS Fat of the spermaceti whale gives the clearest and most
beautiful light of any substance known in nature" nice nature in the
Cantos argue against us all and the words continue to expand like
any universe there is nothing to be done nothing beautiful but still
the boy lingers in the night and thinks the stars might do and
thinks the moon might do and thinks the streetlight might do and
thinks the taillights disappearing redly into the horizon the line
where sky but listen Rilke is still alive no but his friend Balthus is
still alive and they talked one to the other as the stars were heaving
their little lights out into the clueless nights and they learned stuff

and in the eye of one of them the eye of a panther continued to not
blink as if he really saw a panther in a zoo and the image, which is
after all mere light and that itself a matter of dance vibrations
dance is nothing descend into the matter of the beast night-
skinned beast and they spoke into the night as if no one was
listening as the stars shed their skins into the universe great shells
of dancing particles hurtling madly into our eyes yours and mine so
Pound never spoke to me I would not have liked him too cruel
who walked with a stick and banged boys' shins I bet who threw
rocks his way and bottles and Italy kept him what did they know
his Italian better than his Chinese still I wish I had known some
Epic Poet who was alive as if you could tell the difference long they
talk into the night who listens as the crickets or local variety of
noisome insect no not mephitic noisy is all we meant insects kept
their rhythms because they cannot help it any old man's ears will
hear see them any two talking in the dark lost "and those negroes
by the clothes-line are extraordinarily / like the figures del Cossa
Their green does not swear at the landscape 2 months' life in 4
colours ter flediliter: Ityn to close the temple of Janus bifronte the
two-faced bastard 'and the economic war has begun'" crazy about
money he was against it and crazy us we know better we are
perfect money in my youth God loved the poor and we gave coins
with faces on one side and birds on the other and now the poor are
evil you know it anyone can see it in their eyes we don't like failure
anyone the insects the dogs and they are lazy that's the reason my
uncle who could barely read he worked and built his own house of
trash cast off particle board isn't it pretty to think so my uncle did
not like to work either like an artist or philosopher but loved his
coffee and the shade it was the south where shade is an art the
mellifluous chatter of photons will burn blisters into the pavement
the poor live in the shade where there are a few coins remaining
with faces of Roman emperors and whores women who had money
from love never in the sunlight where it burns "and the economic
war has begun" the man said and he called it a poem an epic I was
happy to be alone in those days and would walk down railroad
tracks because there were not many left and the rails were often
rusted think of it the weight of the trains how they shine the rails
and at dusk you could see them for miles the lingering rails
glittering redly on their ties to walk was odd the distance between
ties unnatural a curious dance as the insects hopped across at your

feet you had to keep your eyes down or risk stepping on sharp
stones ballast the round earth moving under your feet the sun as
round as anything from a distance and red think of running here
and jumping into an open car the power at your feet the railroad
fortunes and pointless men jumping on at will at whim sometimes
they fell under the crushing wheels juggernaut oh well and some
had families states and counties distant who I guess never found
out and still the power to just jump on anybody's train when curves
slow them down that was the life those were the days my uncle had
a job and everyboy can work now the unions are going with the
railroads but look at the chicory growing there more blue and
tolerant than the eyes of any democrat a kind woman once spoke
to me she said important things and books could be written and
there are things to do important things and books could be written
and the dust along the road happy or not it is not important was I
happy? perhaps I was happy she gave me a ride it was summer it
was always summer in those years and the dust gave a sense of
delirium to the view the view the horizons were prepared in all
directions I was far from home by foot but not so far in time she
gave me a ride she was kind this was long ago and the world was
only itself she asked for nothing more than I would gladly give later
when the look of those little blue flowers had faded she said it
would make me immortal she was right so far still not such a gift
as one might hope will not pay the rent won't make anyone happy
you can read about it we were always happy when we thought
about we lived that way loving everyone and knowing how to read
Greek for instance or Latin we were better at Latin but Greek was
good for something special and private I mean the old Greek only
the old politics about and beyond the Then Leucothea had pity,
"mortal once Who now is a sea-god: νόστον γαίης Φαιήχων,..."
"What? (The Cantos, 95) can it mean can it matter? Anything can
she taught me that or someone did ...*Odysseus was swept overboard
by a huge wave, and the rich robes which he wore dragged him down to
the sea-depths until his lungs seemed about to burst. Yet being a
powerful swimmer, he managed to divest himself of the robes, regain the
surface, and scramble back on the raft. The pitiful goddess Leucothea,
formerly Ino, wife of Athamas, alighted beside him there, disguised as a
seamew. In her beak she carried a veil, which she told Odysseus to wind
around his middle before plunging into the sea again. This veil would
save him, she promised*—Robert Graves ...*till inundation rise Above*

130

the highest Hills: then shall this Mount Of Paradise by might of Waves
be moovd Out of his place, pushd by the horned floud, With all his
verdure spoil'd, and Trees adrift Down the great River to the op'ning
Gulf, And there take root an Iland salt and bare, The haunt of Seales
and Orcs, and Sea-mews clang. To teach thee that God attributes to
place No sanctitie, if none be thither brought by Men who there
frequent, or therein dwell—John Milton   it is a kind of seagull a
white bird happy above the waves nothing more Have you been
saved? awkward silence awkward salvation at best silence you have
a connection to the kosmos she would say and something smaller
than that something domestic she spoke to him as she cooked she
cradled the telephone he pictured this in that place surrounded by
warmth that place near the throat and cradling shoulder where a
child's face would peer at you as you walked behind the young
mother whose useful body so intrigued you turned you into
something less dangerous less full of the dailyness and anyway she
spoke to me as she blanched the greens and heated oil and I could
hear a knife slice onion and as the imagined molecules formed she
said Have you been saved? and I said Many times and here is room
for more these dangers of the domestic these maternal moments
make me weep ashamedly in the privacy of my own telephone
booth hard it is and how full of fury to be saved to be salvageable it
is a kind of decorum it is necessary in the strictest sense Anyone
can weep can cry real tears it is a trick too easy I believe in
everything everything but nothing can save such unbelief some
bird some passion for air or light or maybe it is god in that form
makes sense withering into light withering like the state slender as
the wind particles pared to feathers and fierce-eyed flight god in
the arrogant air catching a current riding the thermals that's me or
should be a dove a docile form of pigeon short-lived but then she
turned to me her lips on the receiver she turned as if I were over
her shoulder waiting she smiled into the air the electrons and the
little family's dinner hissed think of it of flight and the feather tips
bending with the weave of wind seamews ride behind the garbage
scows filling the air and weak minds with screams delirious with
desire fulfilled filling their sweetening bodies with rotting residue
of whose life mine egg shells parings grease of what small animals
the dead and decomposing of the city followed by the glittery gulls
see them against a sunset let's say why not a touch of romance a
salvation god gathering likely ambiguities into her mouth sharp

131

beaked and belligerent a man a woman encopulant watch all from
their bed the room for rent and nothing is more beautiful nothing
less than saved by all bright gods and tiny temptations save all give
us this day our daily bread and forgive us but day doth daily draw
my sorrows longer and night doth nightly make grief's strength
seem stronger make it new pretend she sings to you pretend she
sings to you she flies to you pretend she flies to you she sings she
dances you need not pretend god dances with you she takes your
hand oh pretend and nothing is more beautiful nothing less saved
by the bright brittle gods their tiny temptations

from

Airs, Waters, Places

(2001)

NO THING

A word that is almost deprived of meaning is noisy. Meaning is limited silence.
        —Maurice Blanchot

Sound as corruption is a further fall, a grace
like wind's incessant pounding, a music as anger—
air belligerent versus a single tree in a field
which is elegance as horizon as curtain drawn
against (any tree in singularity) light and light
whose nobility of patience penetrates the weather:
and from the air, from the airplane I saw
I saw beneath me during that time (I think it was time)
of year I saw the fall of leaves around each tree separate
a powdering of color pastel chalked circle a disk of leaves
and then red and bronze dots and then (we climbed)
the distant earth and then cloud and glitter
as soft in the distance like clouds among
cloud the tree speaking not to me only to itself like God.
Not silent. Nothing is. No thing like it except
surrounds itself with vibrating molecules
known as noise unless it is the susurrant leafage defiant
calling attention, calling. You recall, "Nothing
will come of nothing," said Lear to Cordelia.

WATERY

>whatever is not cannot be
>whatever is cannot not be
>—Anaxagoras

like love the river, no
not like but the river
fills itself, is full, cannot be other

is a river? the water?
full or perhaps empty if
a river is empty is there a river?

beautiful perhaps whether
or not it is, the river
aligned with the bank, lined by

the boundary liminal
fauna the wading birds
beaks shimmer with the river

dripping and the agony—
is it agony to die
a fish down the gullet of a heron?

is a heron beautiful? is
the heron part of the river?
what my mother

called a coulee, through
her childhood her town not
a town it was empty—

is there a town with no
people or dogs?
she and her family

tipped
into the river, the coulee,
their flat-bottomed barge

in the flood
a famous flood
where is the river the land covered

by water the depth
deceptive this
is what it is like to be beautiful

not like but to be
not beauty but necessity
not a river but water

not a heron but
like a heron, long beaked
and full of fish

not flying but wading
not happy but
home

"without figure or fable"

Nietzsche admired Thales admiring clarity (water as father)
water as everything, in its way—the world. As if,
      as pre-Socratic as if my father were—
my father the chemist water taught me titration.
At age eleven I helped him analyze—phenolphthalein
released by drips into the swirling flask we admired the drama
of color change but kept my count cleverly—it is now winter
      far from the lakes of home, the likes of it.
Remember to cry, the clarity of crying,
or cryogenic—no, only frozen, snow only, it drifts
across our vision, it accumulates. Tears.
      Clarity is what we wanted most, lost nothing,
      not simple—the sidewalks do glisten this evening,
the cars pass hissing after rain, after thaw.

Their paired lights litter the walks what is there
to see but what we put there there are many
sources of light few of water   forty years before a father
          loved me in our conspiracy of clarity huddled watching
the color change, the light   shining through the tube
I learned to weigh the color of light against a chart—the shape
of a molecule of water .
          is the shape of those pillows you watch TV
encircled by—reminiscent of a hug the oxygen in the center
          two hydrogen arms extended—
Here join, O welcome, Happy
          conjunction I sit in bed—
          the gray light laps at the window
the light is from the box the TV terrorizing
the center of the unclear the muddle of modern
          life after father, water, wandering fluid flow   hydrodynamics
naval architecture   hoses and drainpipes   gutters
storm drains city streets fountains
hydrants   monthly retention   micturation
          diuresis   irrigation   rain   sleet
snow   drizzle   mist   hail   rainbow
glaze   steam   stream   river
lake   pond   rivulet   sea   bay
          ocean   gulf   canal   channel
mill pond   bayou   coulee   reservoir   swamp
          marsh   the intracoastal waterway offers shipping protection
across the entire Atlantic and Gulf of
Mexico coast a length incalculable a defense

there is no defense

for instance to inventory the riverbed afterward:
doll, clothed
hand mirror, tortoiseshell-backed
spoons
cookery materials, various
Dutch oven, well seasoned
two brooms
an alarm clock, wound
drowned too quickly to ring

138

and the full pathos of a small family
the laughter of waves, wavering
under the long nose of gar

the flat-eyed bass, the perch,
a thin fish, easy to catch
and then at Aswan

a kind of flood
preserved entire
the family tombs and titles

mother peers into the toilet bowl reads dark signs
message from the interior   how many sources?
the breath   the color of urine
the false shapes   who does not accept
a message from anywhere

stars   home   viscera
whence they come, whither they go
mystery behind the flesh beneath the stretched
and sallow skin will kill us in the end, children

and there might have been happiness in the night
a mother-child conspiracy   a man I know
took rouge from the mortician's hand
and himself replaced the color in his dead mother's
cheek pushed the cotton wadding in to fill
the hollows oh gone and glittering mom into the boy's
night peering into the dark remains.

from the poem AGAINST THE CYCLE OF SAINT URSULA
(Carpaccio)

Exaltation of St. Ursula and of Her Companions

In the machinery of injustice
my whole being is Vision
                              —Susan Howe

The strangeness of a strange name cut
from the moorings of association: the word
and the wilderness of it all context. *Siam*
will no longer do. And the rug, even were it
to fly, can no longer be from Persia.

"I have never been anywhere and I plan
to stay home. My mother traveled once
during the war from Washington, D.C.
to San Diego to see my father who,
by the time she arrived dragging my
brother by the hand and swollen full
with me, had sailed into the furious
archipelago of unexploded ordnance,
the alien Asian seas; O adventurous, my father,
and dutiful, fuses and trinitrotoluene
filling his dreams. I like best in life

a good park in spring and the greenness
flowers too and always young mothers
to push babies in spindly machines
the delicate boredom to sit in the shade
to watch and to hum soft loops and whorls
like a fine hand, a practiced hand. Writing."

The hand writing on the wall or the hissing
can of spray. Language abhors a blank wall.
His art did express
A quintessence even from nothingnesse.   (John Donne)

140

In a book who wrote: "Boredom is the dream bird
that hatches the egg of experience"
and then he traveled famously
from Germany during that war
and died by his own hand untimely?

"Yesterday after rain the sun caused a forsythia
to steam, the coolness of the mountain air
and the ultraviolet rays. I expected voices.
The immense effort of Nature is disturbing,
you want to offer it a day off or something.
Anyway I watched a snake-shaped cloud
invade the valley this morning, between
two peaks floating all full of dignity.
The sleepiness below—it *was* early—and lonely.
The trunks of aspen columnar against the sky
are black, but ghostly pale against the mountains.
The dark, wet earth after the storm."
(*Apoteosi della santa*)

SURFACE TENSION

Consider the tear, the silver dis
water—that is me down my cheek,
Or there, in that corner, the child
in pain, but small, harmless pain.
of his own small world, himself
lost, a twin, a sort of

solution of self into salt and
turning cold on my collar.
who weeps machinelike no doubt
not mine. But is. Tearful and fond
examining his happy past
twin.

Reflection is predictable beauty.
bilateral or sometimes bizarre.
On the terrazzo which the crew
with their succulent mops. Or
and a world slowly waves to us
view mirror, glad to see us going.
the city offers, its wind eyes
encouraging, reminding the boy
Clean windows. Glass to keep
outside. The boy in.

Doubling into symmetry,
In mirrors. Car hoods.
has splashed who now caress
a lake when there is little wind
smiling like relatives in the rear-
Or the accidental encouragement
flashing us back at ourselves,
who delights in (endures) the moment.
the world in place. The rain
In the window

the lamp behind you floats
own face doubled
The day will rise, the blonde
the mirroring glass and dim

into the infinite dark, and your
the window mirroring, the night.
twin, the favored one, will dull
the hovering lamp. It means nothing.

in a lake—a litter of leaves
pages—a book in her one hand
her legs must be cold she
above the water—the girl reads
into a kind of love she is

Here: think of a girl standing
surrounds her, she is reading
she is doubled—wavery—radiating—
wears a dress the hemline
what she believes—she reads herself
doubled she is inconsolable.

Those are not tears on the page
marks. Shadows. Those are tears
of water—the lake the clinging
The girl the earth the lake
a film of water, tears, vision
of the world in

those are tears on the page. Water
on the page. That is a splash
world in one of its forms. Liquid.
is like—a tear. You see through
depend upon the bathing
light, the eye in water.

People touch between them is   a layer of darkness a thin skin of no-
light keeping them apart. A world.   To touch is to darken the space
between. The tear is bright, it   glistens, is a lens—the tear
is the girl in light and   the shape the world takes.

from the poem ECHO

Narration As Equivocation

"The moment I remember was when into
my clothes—every buttonhole she filled with blue—
she twined flowers—what could they have been?—
(they were blue, and small, and too
readily at hand) they were the color of eyes,
we tell of such betrayals—the postman arrived, me
(but let's assume such a memory is the lie)
leaning away from her, she absorbed fully in the tree-

Like blossoming of the shape before her, like spring.
Unworthy, I will admit—what blush? who was hurt?
I heard his step and stepped back enduring.
She is gone. A part of someone's life. Perversion
of such moments: dreams, and divisions of my life
into before and after, my past a most faithful wife."

May Such Deception Dismay

Until she died from the stress of it all Brahms carried on his affair with
his best friend's wife, lying "through the teeth," as the Germans say,
letting the world think what it would. His requiem gained a piquancy,
the excitement of the forbidden flaunted; "Oh Clara, how could you!"
he would say to himself, glass in hand, as he watched her stumble home-
ward toward Robert in the washed-out light of another morning, her
figure foreshadowed into dumpiness by the view from his third-floor
window. It was all so abstract, and in its way, such a bore.

Longing for The Present

"A creosoted pole on my property, twenty wires cross there in the corner
of my back yard—but beyond the wires against the dark clouds (not
all clouds are dark) the swallows swoop devouring mosquitoes (assume
they eat mosquitoes) and beyond them the tattered, no, the boiling

edge of weather moves across me—it was such a view of ice-age glaciers moving—if you look straight up—for a few moments, minutes only, the setting sun gives texture and molecular ambiguity to the utility pole, it glows on the western side—and the neighbor's trees their peculiar shade of green leaning into the light—it was Claude Lorraine—it is lower-middle class, it is a world. I live for this.

The clouds mean it will rain but I love the sound of my little lawn sprinkler I will keep it going even if it rains this luxury I insist on I live here.

The tattered edge that cloud, assembling itself boiling itself over again assembling its insouciant dissolving grandeur, deliberate, austere, aggressive cloud. The light will never be just this again, was always this, this is only light."

Having A Past

Mary, the Virgin, encompassed god
held him whole if inchoate—
I held Him in my closed mouth—I believed it so—
he never was but He lay there
in the folds of flesh softer than pillows
behind the sexual apertures
serene in hot grottoes.

Accidental Childhood

I call it luck when a bird's shadow touches me.

It is hard to know things. "Hard" as in the turtle's
shell, the feel of pebbles in the mouth or pocket.

"Every touch is a modified blow"
                    —Ernest Crawley

People believe birds carry danger, disease;
the feel of feathers unlike any other.

145

Little animals cross frequently the backyard.
Sometimes they die—sparrows, a squirrel; once,
a cat. Good children would bury them
in appropriate boxes. The shimmer of its throat, as if cut—
the hollyhocks are a mess, but if there's another
bud which might open, let's leave them.

"Man stands erect, he alone, yet he lays him down, stretched out
quietly for sleep, for love, for death—"
                    —Hermann Broch, *The Death of Virgil*

And what child does not suffer silent and alone? That's
what it means, "child"—a problem and a pathos. Like
Latin the words ran, like chocolate in summer. "How do you
suppose the Romans spoke?" the teacher said, her eyes
unfocused, having said it all already: (Eye, a room—ease as east.)

ON THE SHAPE OF SUCH AS PLANETS, LIKE EARTH

Light expands spherically—fanciful dandelion,
rays and dots, waves and particles—the match lighted and
in half a second a sphere a hundred-eighty-six-
thousand miles in diameter except for the shadows—
a pearl of universe, a place to play to be

this morning in this city the wash of light, the angle
of sunlight is thirty-five degrees—estimate from watching
the old men chase their slow shadows westward
while the young walk north to south, south
to north, their shadows beside them tucked among
the walls and windows—the city threatens

the fyn perl congeleth and wexeth gret of the dew of hevene.
                    Mandeville's *Travels*, chap. xiv, f. 65b

as silver cars swim downstream to the light
then stop. Then start. The buses bellow. The light.
Changes. The sky. A different smell. A scratching
inside the lung of light, inside the eye, against
the cornea. The long morning fills.

And how ridiculous my sight I wipe my eyes
my vision I breathe deeply of a heron stalking
his legs hinge backward his spear-beak
poised even the glitter of his great eye stilled
to more stealthily stalk oh mercy and good-
ness shall follow me.

God, a sphere, round, rejoicing in solitude.
                    Empedocles, Book 1, frag. 135

Pearl is also a color of sky, mother of pearl also.
It hatches in the dark wet oyster it is a daughter
of light of contradiction. Pearl is a shape of rain
and the city shimmers today shivers in gray light
it is a house to kings and counselors of the earth, which
built desolate places for themselves (Job 3:14).

As for the earth, out of it cometh bread, and under it
is turned up as it were fire.
The stones of it are the place of sapphires:
and it hath dust of gold
he said. But what of the light, and then
there are pearls, which rest upon the breasts
of the lovely, and the languishing, and the breath
goes in and out and the pearl warms, and the mother
of pearl is a light laughter, a longing.

Riches and anything that shape the shape
of the earth itself the globe the shape delights
and instructs. The light glints. The shadow
hovers. The bird was once the shape of the egg.
The roundness of anything redeems. And the light.

The fish that makes a pearl at low tide opens
and receives the dew, the stuff of pearls—
it could be so, it was, or was believed so,
congealed dew. The glitter of seawater streaming
off the knobbed and gnarled back of the oyster
the lesson is too wrong for any to resist—
inner versus outer, books and covers,
and who would eat will eat and swallow light.

from

Matter

(2004)

THE TENDER GRASSES OF THE FIELD

When I was a saint I did not have visions but I could see and did note the color of the world—mainly gray, variations on dirt. It's ok, you can live here. The clean sky to attend the child whose hand is empty and mind is muddled.

Consider that earth is made of earth, a mineral and organic amalgam— beyond a tiny range, color is rare. Oh, they will tell you a particular plant, for instance, is red, that certain stars are red, but look for yourself. The color of fox, the color beneath the skin as platelets race, whirling alone in danger, for home.

What won't we do for the sake of the nerves, white threads of agony under the skin, on it, of it… in the wake of remorse we need to pronounce bigger than names. Maybe a verb. Every saint knew how to keep custody of the lips.

The view is lovely, nice sun going, a mountain it goes behind, the mountain made of rock and all. Et in Arcadia Ego, you know. A sheep here or there. A cow. Water. The sound of water if not water. The sound of sheep if not the smell. You call it home.

49 VIEWS OF CHILDHOOD

But he was a quiet child, I was, he was never
one, such a one as would wander

into wilderness alone—untrue, he was
one to play at death as boys will.

I was small when I was small and then
I was no longer. Dolls are delicate. Legs

and arms articulate to sit them
around you and tell them stories, to have them

tell you stories tell him stories make them
up. Dress them. If an end comes

it will come the sky will remain sky
and weather will be simple, simply

where we live during it. Another version
of this world engages these little ones

around us, about our feet, small humans
who have forgotten the future who

splash happily as if weather were a cure
for childhood. We didn't, he didn't, know

better than to sulk heavily as if
I did not watch secretly gathering

clouds, gathering under them
into likely groups—action figures. Us.

It was better when birds did not
gather so forcefully, mournfully back

before ravens and crows had moved
into cities following the pioneer

pigeons—boys walked under groups
would dismally look down, boys and blackbirds

crossing Sunday paths home
back before sparrows would

so cravenly eat from our hands;
children of today know only

small wishes and crooked feet,
articulated legs and artificial voices

to cry Mama or Papa at whim, at the least
tipping of self into horizontal....

They do not see the green sky
we knew then, such empty grandeur:

in silence such insolence, solitude's
reward for being good, which is part

of every eros of childhood. In all parts
of this world there are children

except in the coldest southernmost,
Antarctica as imagined goal, to gather

there his dolls, my wish, his need
for clean weather and snow

articulated weather; is there no
child to sleep on that continent?

No child's dream floated ever above
the white horizon of an ice containment

bends the bodies to its will,
makes a wish. Like birds

the bodies fit in the fist. The still
children play those little games

the birds of the air the lilies
of the field, the insolence of the whole

agon; suicide as self expression
is paradox, as is sex as self. He made

little houses for his dolls to sit
through afternoons to peer

out narrow windows and be
invisible to have things to see.

I have, he has, things to say, he has
he had things. To say he was

a boy belonging to the end
of habitation, health and happiness.

If this doll could sin she would sing
to him I would sing also, to her

is it like forsythia, logical because
the branch wavers and blossoms bloom

while wind does what wind will?
A dance is like this: to console

as to clasp these hands, touch there
in the air away from bodies

and then to angle the arms, turn
the hips and some part submerges

drowned as the doomed self would
like voodoo, dolled up and doomed—

dancing anyway ever. He could sing
and does deliberately, the child, it

follows that anguish is not me,
nor do we suffer who make those cries.

He would drown his dolls slowly
slide into agonized waters

which reflect the intricate lace
of the bridge which trembled above

them, a bridge which fell in the end
vortex shedding and resonant

oscillations, a dance the bridge did
with the air, not the words the wind

is the reason for suffering. A past
is anything's childhood is a reason

flares into mind like burning
burning which might have been

mind, a doll could have one
and could dance like anything.

WHERE THE FAMOUS WISH THEY HAD LIVED

Parmenides of Elea

Where his influence could accumulate, where the horizon might retreat, where the basilisk smiles and the necessary arrogance of desire lingers into evening while yet hiding among the hieroglyphs. But I like it this way, he said to himself. Here shall I close my trustworthy speech and thought about the truth. Henceforward learn the beliefs of mortals, giving ear to the deceptive ordering of my words, he said. He watched stars move a certain way, the small sprinkling of the past he walked beneath when he was out late and lingering.

In a land of ha-has and paths of desire. Where Nothing hovers invitingly above the closest horizon. Between the angles of incidence and of reflection. Among the agonies in the garden. Elsewhere.

Sigmund Freud

"If his lips are silent, he chatters at his fingertips; betrayal oozes out of him at every pore." And yet looking into the mirror otherwise known as morning otherwise known as night was not a revelation to him. He had a path, strewn with candy wrappers, or flowers, and lined with stones, which was a comfort to him when his throat ached and his head betrayed him. Still wouldn't it have been good to stop in at some familiar coffee shop, to order in a childhood language a childhood treat, something with chocolate and a little something to soothe the guilt which follows from having hoped too fervently and made all those promises. A place where the libraries do not contain your own books and the children are not afraid. Memory, remember, is a dynamic process like the eloquence of birds and the kinds of cancer which affect the jaw. The cave of the mouth from which words emanate, and breath. "I am still out of work and cannot swallow," he wrote after the first of his thirty-three surgeries.

Emil Kraepelin

"In dream I was a child—*childhood* is our myth of psychiatry, but children continue to live in dream—being chased across a landscape. I was not afraid—there is no fear in such landscape—but I did hurry. I would live there where there are no shadowy mountains, where rivers are slender gleams and cold, where the grasses vastly sound through the evening, sounding of air known as wind, felt—but there was a barrier, a glass wall under which a child's body might fit, but not his head. There is no child in this world but in the world of dream I want to live there, there on the other side. I want to live in someone else's dream, any healthy child's. I will live in any body."

WORK IN SILENCE

Wie beurteilt Einer, Welches seine
rechte und welches seine
linke hand ist? Wie weiß ich,
daß mein Urteil mit dem der
Andern übereinstimmen wird?

How does one determine
which is his right hand and
which his left hand?
How do I know my judgment
will agree with another's?
— *Wittgenstein*

My right handed mother cuts
paper patterns
paper my mother in the night cutting
patterns my sister wearing paper
in the night the needles glitter

the pins hold the paper on my sister
her body
she wears
herself in the night holding
in the night a writing
a darkening delivers us
a darkness then a dawn

they work through the night there is urgency
they are clothed in urgency it is their work in the night
they speak rarely the rustling of the paper could be the sound
of the words printed thereon words on my sister
on the paper she wears and dotted lines and arrows

a thin figure I
read long into the night I cut
paper strips of paper I read

someone puts paper into the tree onto the trees
in the night the trees bloom paper long
strips white nothing more beautiful streams
like tears in the night like light

we should make sounds we should use air
to make sounds you hold the mouth this way
you breathe out through it it usually works
there is a name for it

see here her
hand like light descends
below it a shadow ascends
see they touch

not a shadow it is
her other hand sinister
the needle pierces

the other hand receives
no word my mother speaks
nothing to the other hand to come
receive

my sister's dress the fabric
like air moves with air
the air breathes this dress
it is light

and two blades converge
the sound they make is a hiss
a small shrillness the scissors
a mirroring against the paper first
like Narcissus the blade touching itself

—a mirror the window has become
it shows the boy himself
me my face breathing there are no
words coming out of it—

desperate to reach its other self
then the cloth to cut the tiny cry

some old air still
caught in her wings she
balances awkward looking but
balanced
it is a morality a way to let live

how the word "believe" works is
you accept the unstated penumbra
of impossibility and then con
struct there a camp of consolation
in other words
in the house
angelic as if the hierarchy held
as in held water
something between Man and God, Mom
as if any word were
tenderly merciful—man—god—mom

what woman could live there her winged
wisdom bearing her onward
her uses of air : to breathe :
to swim in, as if : to shape glittery :
to hold in trust a shape until it returns

in the night their four hands wing shaped
I see them reflected in the window
against the dark air waiting

or here is the other mode to appraise and approach:
the house as a kind of box and form of failed weather
it is warm for instance or cold it contains us all boy
girl mother at some time or other we live there it is
home and some are away from home and some have
never been home and some move forever as if the
fullness of time were our roof the fall our foundation

ORIGAMI

Consider how little a thing
it is, her hand.
How nothing is sufficient
but everything is necessary.
Wings, for instance.
Handkerchiefs. Umbrellas.
Folded things. Her hand
an enclosure. A secret space
enacted in the flesh, a false
interior. A touch.
And yet it is anguish to know
something about anyone, to feel
with one's own hand the hollow
bones so near flight. No one
can close his eyes on this:
a wonder, willfully offered
as if nothing, a mere mereness,
a trifle like a fan unfolding
of paper oiled to translucency.
Her skin was not transparent
only his breath upon it.

ON THE ORIGIN OF LANGUAGE

People longed to "understand"—come to terms with, we might now say—their unhappiness, which made them different from the not-unhappy animals around them. These not-unhappy creatures seemed to mock the struggling humans who, once they came into language, invented happiness and with it, a kind of childhood.

Another theory is that language invented the human by a mechanism not yet well understood. "Happiness" seems in this theory to play a catalytic role, not as fact but as conceptual possibility.

Finally there is the suggestion that the pressure of consciousness began to be too painful to remain merely interiorized, hence the process of exhaling was over time modified into a release not only of carbon dioxide and the fetid gaseous products of the decaying internal organs, but a release also of the parasitic entity best understood as "thought," or "arrogance," or "interior necessity."

THE NAMING OF SHADOWS AND COLORS

1. Things that Cast Shadows

How the world is gentle in that
whatever can be taken must be shared,
such as umbrage; and the light
can be in your eyes or the shadow
on the page in such a way as obscures
the shape—casts shadows, detaches surface,
the varieties of shade seduce:
afraid of the shadows of doubt, of
my own dreams, yet I know dreams too
have names yet I cannot recall: Do
I dream in color? The color of the world
is the skin, isn't it—bound and bounded
trying always to escape itself, that was
the dream the world had, I had dreamed
it had a shape, a shade and semblance
…semblances and thin shapes of things   *De Rerum Natura,*
are thrown off from this outer surface   Lucretius
the sincerity of surface suffices as
dream is a shadow cast by Mind
shading into itself, the little mind
making itself seem large in hope of frightening
itself into resolution; then dream is a kind
of color that light distorts, dissolves, discards.
But color is light, is the behavior of light
in the world. What is there to love
but the world, its things and shades and
matter. Let us love the names: what
is the name of this world? Space.
What is the name of the other world?
Time. What is the name of the light?
Color. What is the name of color? Change.
Image, as Lucretius contended,
is continuous, a crumbling into infinity

of everything, wave upon wave
of everything, gentle because too thinned
to threaten, attenuated everything…

The story used to be told, Pliny told
the story, lovely, of Dibutade
outlining her lover's shadow on the wall
the night before he went to war. No one
tells stories anymore. No one casts shadows.
What did Pliny love? A good story. A story
is shadow cast by event, or by doubt,
or a story is the color of the absence
of the heroine, she who tacked the shadow
onto the wall, for instance.

Naturalis Historiae,
XXXV, 151-2

My older brother, who became an engineer and helped men walk on the
moon took photography classes as a child I watched and listened his
teacher made my brother make a pinhole camera (I made one secretly
myself, the salt-box and tinfoil taped slyly into technology, a kind of
making like love.) & by the time they got to enlarging I saw the darkroom
duties as an identical process backwards—these men organized light
to send along a lensed new path to collide with silver halides all light
informed…. Although the structure of the AgBr and AgCl lattice
is face-centered cubic, an enormous variety of crystal shapes can be
obtained, depending on the number and orientation of twin planes and
the conditions during growth…the crystals in commercial emulsions
usually contain mixed halide phases. Films suitable for a hand-held
camera generally contain silver bromoiodide, in which iodide ions are
incorporated into the AgBr lattice during crystal growth.
www.kodak.com/US/en/corp/researchDevelopment/

And here is a story told of things:
that the thing names itself like for instance
when that other dream comes into your room
and pesters you for your things, all things,
as if things were lesser entities, smaller
than their colors, thicker than their shadows.
So I talked with her, my friend, who knows
Japanese, and asked her how to say things
what it might be like to say things as if

the shadow of my thoughts were cast across
half a world, the source of shining,
the orient, the language of the rising
sun (but see
how the word refers to resemblance,
"oriental topaz"—look it up)

...so many words, too, are pronounced alike.
"Kinkai" means "a gold bar," "the coastal waters,"   Malinda Markham
and "it gives me great pleasure (to do that for you)."

"Suited to simple races, peasants, and savages"
Le Corbusier—not his real name—said of color
which he found on his journey to the east.
Me, I like them all, all colors, shading
into each other, you know, the spectrum,
a spectacle of itself, oh like a ghost. Specter,
inspector Ball provides the names:

verditers: artificial copper blues
Mars colors: artificial iron oxides   Philip Ball,
lake pigments: from fabric dyes   *Bright Earth*
white—titanium dioxide
cinnabar—mercury sulfide (red)
cinnabar—blood of dragons and elephants—*According to Avicenna the*
dragon wraps his tail around the legs of the
elephant, and the elephant lets himself sink   Bartholomew
upon the dragon, and the blood of the dragon   Anglicus,
turns the ground red; and all the ground that   *De proprie-*
the blood touches becomes cinnabar...   *tatibus rerum*

Let's have it so. A good story

(*tolle lege, tolle lege* spoken in a sing-song voice by
an unseen child from behind a wall, according to Augustine)

whose riper abundance deserves the world's
gaudy spring, whose tender Pity might never
die, a famine of the grave, fairest bright memories,
(from light's waste to sweet bright eyes

increase desire, self-substantial fuel—
gaudy the world, or else glutton: too cruel:
here are other names and things:
yellow ochre, ferric hydroxide
red ochre, Fe_2O_3, ferric oxide
heat yellow ochre and get red ochre
hydrate red ochre and get yellow
from the madder, a flower,
$C_{14}H_6O_2(OH)_2$, alizarin
$C_{14}H_5O_2(OH)_3$, purpurin.
They named the rainbow Iris.

A shadow of some former self,
down Ursulines Street thirty years later I
glimpse again—like a dream of stone—
the garden through the gate (if a hand
goes through, a gate, if not, a door)
as if in pity. As if pitied? Piety.
Pity the world, or else this glutton be,
To eat the world's due, by the grave and thee…
a vision of cloistral shade and floral
lined walks, a place forbidden but there,
in sight, temptation to our better nature:
From fairest creatures we desire increase.

2. Things that Have Color

THING [[ME < OE, council, court, controversy,
akin to GER *ding*, ON *thing* (orig. sense, "public
assembly," hence, "subject of discussion, matter,   *OED*
(how odd these ways of making words
have surface, to cast a form of selves upon
the page like the pen eroding into ink,
like shadows of the thinking that survives)
thing") < UE *tenk-*, to stretch, period of time <
base *ten-*, to stretch > THIN]]

If we scrutinize closely what is done in counting an
aggregate or number of things, we are led to consi-
der the ability of the mind to relate things to things,
to let a thing correspond to a thing, or to represent a
thing by a thing, an ability without which no think-
ing is possible.

Richard
Dedekind,
*Meaning
of Number*

Fast Color. Fast, as in the desert for forty days
and nights. How speedy the fast are, the girls
we admired in high school. Fastened to no one,
they were themselves and loved. Feast.

In a certain drawing by Tibaldi there is no wound
no place for the hand to insert itself. Hand made
belief, manufactured faith. Anyway, belief being
handy enough, a ready relief from the stress
of waiting for the tomb to open. After all it is
Easter today, is it not—the day I write.
This tree here, see outside my window, this
tree is full to bursting of its own efflorescence,
I see the embarrassed little knobs and
buds so full of their own sexuality oh
don't look, give it a little privacy.

What color will it be, this bloom when
the skin cracks and the petal emerges,
and what emergencies we have known
in their shadow necessities, there.

So this apostle wanted a place
to put his hand, to touch to taste to see
the wound. Wounds R Us this season,
this is spring, it says here. You
can hear the breaking bark
see the little cracks forming hear
the invisible screams as the flesh parts,
tears, molecular disintegration. It bleeds
itself into season. Who doesn't.
Touch the torn places.

"Mummy hand with amulets (human hand and
blue-glazed pottery, Late Period"—   The Field
—says something in sign,   Museum
the hand, I believe, the fingers. But in Egyptian.
Elsewhere another boy disregards the Saint—
a book in his sinister hand his severed tongue
in his right, severe witness to his own faith   "St. Romanus of
his own wound—below the boy's throat cut   Antioch," Art
in paint, Zurburan, a kind of story telling.   Institute of
Everyone talks too much given half a chance.   Chicago
Dumfounding, such stillness observed, a moment—
let us observe a moment of silence. What color is it?

3. Words Neither Cast Shadows Nor Have Color

Easter Monday, 2002:
All that was hidden is revealed,
and sometimes the thing was chocolate,
yet mostly you see the shattered shells
discarded, peeled off but reconstructable
of the boiled egg, the colors dizzying,
the sad detritus of the body of the res.

Shadow, shame and hand-tinting all have their
effects on how we say it: once the poets were first
and the painters to follow, to make only
what had been named: "Line drawing   Pliny
was invented by the Egyptian Philocles or by the   XXXV, 16
Corinthian Cleanthes, but it was first practiced by
the Corinthian Aridices and the Sicyonian Telephanes—
these were at that stage not using any color, yet already
adding lines here and there to the interior of the
outlines; hence it became their custom to write
on the pictures the names of the persons represented."

"Maple leaves are often used to convey the idea that you have been jilted. The Japanese word for Maple leaves and love being *iro*—a subtle reference to changing colour."

C.G. Holme, *Glimpses of Old Japan*
from Japanese Colour Prints: Birds
and Flowers (London, 1936)

"Iro" does mean color, though: "Kami" is "paper," and
"irogami" is "colored paper." "Cha" is "tea," and "chairo"
is "brown" (tea-color). "-ppoi" is kind of like our "-ish,"
and "iro" with "ppoi" attached to it (iroppoi) means "sexy,"
especially for women. "Colorish," in a way, but only non-
Japanese would hear it like that. If you put the same
"iro" with the character for "woman" or "man," it
means a lover. But "maple leaves" is just "momiji."

"Since the beauty of a Japanese print is mainly that of lines, straight or curving, broad or slender, I do not see why a carver's knife is not at its best in nude studies. The reason why, unlike the Greeks, we did not venture to find the highest symbol of art in the human form, should be discovered in social ethics, more than anything else, which taught us how to transform life's falsehood into a hyperbole of superficial arabesque beauty.

The Ukiyoye Primitives,
Yone Nocuchi (Privately Printed,
Nakano, Tokyo, 1933) p.107.

What have you named yourself?
Is it a secret? Is it dangerous?
Who is allowed to choose her own name?
What would your mother think?

The name of the species is a place
to start. Not a place. The birds he named
were sometimes wrong, the names, but
his pictures were of something—of the young
of the Whooping Crane, he named
Sand Hill Crane. I traveled there once,
Nebraska, the Sand Hills. I was late and the birds
would speak in the twilight, a kind of murmuring
loud and it had to do with sleep.

I would sleep, too, after the drive
from Chicago. There is a city in Colorado
not my destination, named Ovid.

Is there a place you practice
pronouncing this name, secretly? Is it
safe? Is it the same name in the dark
as in the light? Does it fade during the day?
Can you pronounce it backward?
Can you say it in your mind so loudly
it hurts? Can you live without it?

Audubon's Feliciana Sketchbook, 1821 to 23,
contains flying things mostly, not birds,
Praying Mantis, Spider, Fly, for instance,
this mantis was circus pink, the fly as if
dressed in blue-checked abdomen. The spavined
spider, full of venomous threat, gray and
yellow, enlarges on the page—I do not believe
he knew its name. I think he lied here,
made it up as if with his eyes closed. Spider.
We must love such a world.
Among us still, they are elegant all,
pink and gray and blue. Ovidian charm—
those he named, like Arachne, like Picus.
Every name is holy. Hollyhock
whose lower leaves waver lacy with rot or
chewed into delicacy. It takes a little time for
the charm of the hollyhock as an adolescent scatter
of self into the willing world, tipping over
still standing florally abundant,
thickly raucous and weedish.

Or can it ever matter again who
tends the garden now that longing has deflected
itself into itself, selfish, now that the little ones
bask in the light, the litter of insect bodies
gathers nightly underfoot, under purple waves?
I prefer the moth, the bulge
of body awkward against the grace of wing;

who flies under moonlight and gathers
grace into himself, eats the flowers, or perhaps
(the gray insignificant) eats the clothes
off our backs, under our feet the wool
of our carpets. The good moths eat anything,
in one of their forms. Fancy. We have a world
we love one another. We can fly
in the dark, enough dark, desiring.
I am thinking of History, which is a way
to name time. The name of this year,
for instance. To be allowed, from *laudere*,
to praise. To name is to praise is
a trick of words, all words are tricks.
A picture is worth thousands. *Pingere,*
ut pictura poesis. Time absolves
everyone everything. Give it
time. Solves all problems. Loses,
sits it out. He made other sketchbooks
of flowered weeds and wilderness,
of every horned and horrific creature
he might see. Beast. That is a name.
Yours? Truly.

from

Tendril

(2007)

TEA PARTY

There remain whispers. These were, are.

These are errors, terrors, he said. To himself, whispered.

[To Be Sad Safely]

A man named Henry Tuke in 1796 established a madhouse. His
son Samuel (1784-1857) was interested in the conditions of the insane
and wrote a book, *Description of the Retreat* (1813), which had great
influence in reforming treatment. Samuel Tuke's son also entered
the family business and aided in the management of the York Retreat,
which became famous for Samuel's use of kindness and high tea,
teaching his mad to indulge as the conventions required. When a
patient could properly behave at tea, he was released.

There are so many uses of the mouth, the teeth and tongue—a portal
of sorts, sorting the airy from the earth, the watery, dispensing and
receiving in turn. We make of used air a sound and in turn speak, chew,
swallow, choke, tremble on the glassy edge and hope we did it well, well
enough, to enter the world, we would say. Like any creature trembling.

Trifles, truffles on the plate, seduction and a kind of medication, a
kindness, can save us?

Thomas Wyatt (1503-1542) wrote:

That now are wyld, and do not remembr
That sometyme they put theimself in daunger
To take bred at my hand; and nowe they raunge
Besely seking with a continuell chaunge.

A word a small wind—notice
some outside my window,
beside some silence, appalls: white white
it might be saying, the words
                    I see move

175

a green limb, evidence of wind
winding through the glass
the window, wind eye, here beside me.

                              They flee
from me that some time did me
seek he said (I said of apparitions that they fly
when something comes, morning)
cloudless mourning. Dissipative,
susurrant, strange fashions for forsaking—

why it matters, whether matter enters—
Why it—Thomas, he was the doubter
and yet could be a saint in spite—
matters to take tea or not, perform according
to formula and not spill—enters—

and not fear and not fear.

Beside himself in various ways the world too much
with us who have passed the halfway point—like
leaves which do fall but not ill,

they accumulate in the fall, we rake them but
can no longer burn with impunity so the bonfire
of our children makes us wince.

                         Windows onto
something, the only thing the only sound
to penetrate: a spine of self and sound,
a spiral of hollow bones align a sort
not spill a thing anything will do, we
are such creatures

as dreams are spilled on. Nightmare,
lente, lente, currite noctis equi
someone sad said. Of?
It was no dream. I lay broad waking.

They fle from me that sometyme did me seke
he said and he was waking broad and loved
like anyone this life, he took what he could
and gave back more, was happy.
Why not.

[Enter Eros]

When her loose gowne from her shoulders fell
was there a man could see and not feel fall
the gown as if a curtain drew a slight aside
a sight a way it did it was and showed
a meaning for matter that was
beyond what was and could be later
when her loose gown from her shoulders fell?

And she me caught in her armes long and small.

But she didn't and it is fear I feel
falling from her shoulders like a gown
and flesh is falling from her shoulders like
a gown and fear is falling to my shoulders
like, shameful full of fury
my own head leaking the excretion
of my fear my dark shoulder showing
oh my silly fear will kill me.

To fear and fear and face it at the table
cup of tea in hand and others shoulder
to shoulder round we celebrate the day
the end the after noon with tea and say
the proper things and like to love each
the other apparition and despair desire
sitting on plates little cookies chew
there is fear to count on waiting humble
in our rooms to return to seek, bare of foot
and shoulder small and smiling all.

What is broken, what is whole, is
if you can touch it it will break. If it can touch you
it is whole. If it is it is, isn't it, or: we met
over tea on a veranda, looking out over—not
at each other, there was a landscape—looking out
over the steeply declined land and there
was a ribboned gleam below, of course, the course
of a simple river gleaming in the last of the lingering
sun, the kind of setting poems arise from, like mist
missed from the river which, in spite of its shimmer
is less river than rivulet, riven by land, the dirt declining
into, dissolving in, solving into itself. We resolved
never to taste that river, that water, water that was
has been so solved, so used to dissolve the lingering
issues of mist like a little landscape watched we did
didn't we, not each other but the little sun going we
watched sitting as we were side by side touching
(we cannot recall possibly our shoulders touched)
each the other, the warmth of the warmer one
draining into the cold or colder flesh of the other,
but we cannot recall and no longer break.

THE LAST DAYS OF GÖDEL

What counts in a life? If its end
is terror, this tendency numbers have to combine
into mind, to add themselves all unheeding
into the new, the no longer numerous.
Arithmetic is thought
to occur in the left cingulate gyrus.
A mapped brain a geometry: Mind,
a closed system, can know what it knows

of itself only by what it knows of itself. Gödel
showed we cannot know what we know.
No, what we don't. *Whose only wish was that*
death come as soon as possible
without causing any trouble to others,   Gaisi Takeuti,
his friend wrote. *There was no grief, no sorrow.*   *Memoirs of a*
What consumed him was such a nihilistic despair   *Proof Theorist*
that it could scarcely be called despair.

His brother Rudolf remembered the rumor
wandering ghostlike the Brünn Gymnasium
that Kurt committed no errors
in four years of Latin—a closed system   not only was his
complete, a sanctity—like the virtue   Latin given top marks,
inedia—begs to fill appetite, a failing.   but...he had made not
It was rumored   a single grammatical
                                                  error   —Rudolf Gödel

He predicted his own death three times: in nineteen
forty-six, in nineteen seventy, and finally
correctly in nineteen seventy-eight. He starved
himself for fear of poisoning. When he walked
his feet would break through and find a falling.
Thin ice.

        Attention wavers;
the water to walk on   glitters;
a wash of sun   on skin   a recompense

even as gathering damage warns—who doesn't
need warnings   ice is a grammar
a thin film on chaos, words, churning

in a past his little
triumphs glitter watery or mirage.
Beckon him back. A little life
was not enough, still he will not move
but feels a light
particular caress.

Furthermore, when his wife returned from his funeral,
a burglar had broken in and jewelry and other goods
had been stolen. I felt then
resentment against modern   Gaisi Takeuti
times as well as American society.

Consider a hand on your back:
his best hand takes your right hand and
both feel the day descend piece by piece
a cumulation of catastrophes
huddled in the light—

your skin exceeds you.
To have touched some skin
a skin upon itself then a body beneath
when we walk our feet break through and find
a fallenness: *who will live his life?*

His skin prepared itself
for proofs: geometry for the weak,
logic for the strong. A skin is surface.
Any page will do.

Making a science of my own bad mind
I learned to know a world, any world, again;
not as it could or should be but as a thing
of parts rewarding the one to piece a theory
but not back, not again, always afresh—

to be a big boy among little teams
and learn a means to quantify lack.

As proof they offer to learn a kind
of kindness, a drifting calculus
to interpret stones; among the numbers
only trust the average, all types of time

summarized and simulated, the appalling
will to know emergent, the felt recalling.

The thridde point of Theorique, Which cleped is Mathematique,
Devided is in sondri wise… The ferste of whiche is Arsmetique,
And the secounde is seide Musique, The thridde is ek Geometrie,
Also the ferthe Astronomie.   John Gower, *Confessio Amantis*

Do not leave the mark of your body in bed.
Never pluck a garland. Do not eat beans.
Avoid that which has fallen. Never stir the fire with
iron nor eat from a whole loaf. Do not eat the heart.
Do not walk on highways. Do not let swallows live
under your roof. When you remove a pot from the fire,
do not leave its mark in the ashes. There were many
rules for the Mathematekoi, who lived with the Society,
had no possessions beyond the body and learned from
Pythagoras himself.

What counts?

Luck and

in fall leaves turn charming colors
& maybe there is distance made visible

a physical thing like a future—

the long afternoon is a sin
of years on spindles,
a piling up mathematical out of legend,

the one about the end of the world

gold light settles onto the diamond needle;

an elaborated set, rules the luckiest learn.

What counts?

through your window watch
whatever falls
fall.

Herein lies his fame, his Incompleteness Theorem
which simply says If system S is consistent
we cannot prove it within itself; S and the proposition
"S is inconsistent" is consistent. The consistency
of axioms cannot be proved.

Herein lies his fame: he was a thin man
who distrusted food, which is to say the world
which was discontinuous with his body
and like any saint, S, would be unprovable
to himself his slender self infinitely regressing.

Herein lies his fame: he erased himself;
the null set, the sadness infinite and pale

After his death, his last days lingered in my mind.   Gaisi Takeuti
Why should the last days of Gödel have been like this?

SAD HOUSES

If some small mind among mountains asserts
a self (any self will do) and makes a home of height,
then it *says* a self out of hope and fair weather.

But weather is where we, in the end, live, and nothing
will do but to bend to it, and anyone's child is worth
dying for given circumstance, if you stand around long enough

you'll find some life to save, from drowning in something,
then if it is still day and the sharp angled peaks do not block
the sun the light will change, the trees will cast

shadows and point the way, a way, houseward, home.
I do live in this world's words, and those regrets did
follow me here, among mountains, the wildering

of place in the evening where nothing
substantial remains for long unbent.
Call it a kindness.

Delusions, hallucinations, agitation, blunted affect, social withdrawal, apathy,
anhedonia, poverty of thought, poverty of speech content; affects the most
fundamental human attributes including language, perception and sense of self

Particle physics: the search for that which is only itself
and is not a randomness
not statistical terror.

For there is a dream from the adversary which is terror.
For the phenomenon of dreaming is not of one solution, but many.
                    (Christopher Smart, *Jubilate Agno* (fragment B, 3)

.

Here is what I learned: a thing—a house, for instance—is generated
when matter (for instance, if you make a house, timber, nails, sheetrock,
tubes and tendrils of copper) is arranged according to form (a plan,

blueprinted architectural, for instance) so when form dissolves matter
might remain, but no house, no place to return homeward. *An animal
is generated when matter (contributed by the mother) combines with form
(contributed by the father).* His theory, he wrote, and meant it, Aristotle.
Not mine, but meaning is meaning, take it, I said to myself.

*For the changeableness of changeable things is capable of all those forms to
which the changeable are changed. And what is this? Is it soul? Or body? If
it could be said: "Nothing: something that is and is not," that I would say…"*
here's a saint confessing, but does it help and who wouldn't say it, that all
is and is not?

The clouds were, and daffodils, and the work he did—now no more.
His life, health and happiness. The weather, too, it is and isn't.

The known world's anguish increases, mentally creased and spindled—
how odd that *anguish* has nothing to do with angle—to bend, as a
fishhook…the words I mean.

*Forming connections with the cerebral cortex, white matter and
brainstem, the limbic system is involved in the control and expression
of mood and emotion, in the processing and storage of recent memory,
and in the control of appetite and emotional responses to food*

Well, and who doesn't love this summer weather?
But some do prefer the darker comforts
of hearth and the need for
and some prefer to walk
unswept autumnal
and some change their names
hoping to find one that fits
and a more savage substance
the body, fishlike, dangling
give it a name, a name

Bathed in tears the eye tries,
we have made the air dirty, and the water,
which is our house but we feel clean in our hearts
or no, we don't, we feel besieged and therefore

184

no longer look, "heart" being a metaphor in this case
for…we have forgotten. Necessity, perhaps.

No, "heart" has a long history of abuse. I mean the word,
but also the organ. Bathed in blood the organ beats
its low tune for a lifetime, then retires… we look there
or would look there, in there, except that the air
is dirty, and the water, and evening is far, and the morning,

even if in opposed directions, and as in swimming a river
the halfway point is where it does not matter what choice
we make, to return or to continue, is of heart, unhoused.

from the poem TENDRIL

et in Arcadia ego

Her House

I am the one satisfied with sadness,
summer on the river, her last house unlivable
(loved?) a wasp hive in the bird feeder a hive unhidden

a now-clouded plastic (to feed birds)
(a tube attached to the window) from
the kitchen a view of a lawn strewn
with calcium carbonate (not chalk,

limestone, cave stalactites, coral, or pearls) oyster shells
from her hen house, snakes in the nest box—

still this is landscape, still life: a torn scatter,
trees at the edge of woods seen from the road
a horizon broken...all is broken

yellow swirl in the green of rice are
the tops of crawfish traps in flooded fields
various shades of gray and blue varied angles

of light—a textured wall a grain silo an evening

—a house to be broken a life too, soon

a second storey of a house complete, the first
story walls washed away all
tatters remain against posts and studs

(no, see—I saw this, the house standing
but the walls by the storm away   taken
a kind of neatness to it, unkindness)
the line of debris in the trees at twelve feet
the high the water at its highest a horizon
white trailers, hundreds ranks and rows among
a kind of wild hibiscus spider lilies
nests with herons   herons stand sentinel in nests

in trees along the road dense crowds of white and blue,

⎯⎯

(the former Louisiana heron
now tricolor) and cattle egrets

camellias, the smell
the barn house the pump house
water   rice   sugar cane
biplane flying, helicopter at rest
horses   sheep   goats
caterpillars crossing the roads

mirages and red wing blackbirds on the pavement
cormorants an alligator dead on the highway
Cameron, Calcasieu, Jefferson Davis, Vermillion
these the names of Parishes: Latin *parochia*, from
Greek *para* + *oikia* = "a temporary staying"
(para, paradise, paranoid, etc.)

Indecent, the delicate exposure
of roots, pine and oak and other, torn great holes

⎯⎯

in the mud then dry white soil but now new rain
new larvae the mosquitoes drive us off the land
into her house where she has lived Faulknerian
thirty years in cool semidarkness
cannot speak nor swallow, tubed, ticking
clock-like forward into silence. She writes me notes.

Elegant analyses offered by wind thus
wilderness is one result, an end like an art form
the long walk homeward.

The wild deer-ness of the days and dense
city only distant, fair gossamer presence
our kind reward—the palpable
sensory, sensible night's eros.

. . . .

Tendril (A)

In the fall of that year I noticed a piece of a Roman wall now on display
in the museum. A relief panel in plaster. A bit of white plaster had been
molded in the form of a winged female figure alighting on a tendril, set
against the dyed blue wall while still wet, the figure alighting between two
deer. She, the winged one, holds in her hand an offering to the deer she
faces, a gesture reminiscent of the angel by Klee who offers a little breakfast.

The wings are faintest curves, a series of streaks of plaster almost
accidental. Love the accidental. The almost accidental. I could call those
wings Aspects of Grace. They are not attached. They are suggestions.

Her curved body carved; to carve, a graph, engraved in plaster…

Seduction. I do not know if she is human, intended to depict the human
form.

The Buddha and Heraclitus were contemporaries. The suggested curve
between them in place and time. Only time.

I began making sketches of her, and her deer come to feed, in my notebook. I returned every day to make another awkward, personal version of a winged female figure alighting on a tendril. Some days I would get the line of the back, some days I would be able to imitate the wings. Never the entire figure.

As a boy I fell in love with a figure, a girl in a radio drama about a scientist who developed a microscope more powerful by a factor a thousands than any then known. In a drop of water through his lens he discovered a city in which lived a girl. As he watched the scientist fell in love then watched her writhe in agony and die as the drop evaporated. I had my own radio, my first transistor model. I listened to the story in the dark of my room.

An answer as an unfolding. To speak, for instance, to a figure with wings, and then to see the wings begin unfolding, as your answer. As in, "I love you" and she unfolds her wings to leave you.

Plicare. Replicate. Plait. Pleat.

I tried drawing her and am no artist. I filled a book, and then another.

Replicatory can mean, "of the nature of a reply."

I am no longer a child. Once we took our son to a little "nature museum" in Colorado. A tame deer followed us. We petted her, and were all of us humans shocked at how hard the hide was, how course the hair. Her little hooves were delicate, brutal.

Jean Cocteau adopted for his signature a five-pointed star, which he copied from the scar on Apollinaire's face. Cicatrix. Cocteau visited Apollinaire in the hospital—one of the Corporal Acts of Mercy.

———

algebraic curve: a curve expressed by an equation containing only algebraic functions, i.e. such as involve only addition, multiplication, involution, and their converses; of which kind are the various conic sections:

opposed to *transcendental* (or *mechanical*) *curve*, one which can be expressed only by an equation involving higher functions, as the catenary, cycloid, etc. *curve of probability*: a transcendental curve representing the probabilities of recurrences of an event. *curve of pursuit*: the curve traced by a point moving with constant velocity, whose motion is directed at each instant towards another point which also moves with constant velocity (usually in a straight line). *curve of sines*: a curve in which the abscissa is proportional to some quantity and the ordinate to the sine of that quantity; so the curve of cosines, tangents, etc. See also Anaclastic, Catenary, Caustic, Cubic, Exponential, etc etc. (OED)

Tender

like small rain on the tender
herb she did
alight and here or there
is nothing to be done a moment's
monument to, all monumental,
days accrue and nights,
consolations of offending vision…she did
stand near but unaware which
was dear to him, his sight, who watched
for hope even of a tree cut down   Job 14:7
that it will sprout again and that
the tenderest branch will not cease,

tender to only his mother, his century
not peaceful, his century a serious
deficiency, like memory.

Tendril (B)

I listened to the story in the dark in my room. I suppose I cried. Children do.

"Replicate" can be pronounced several different ways—one of these, as an adjective, can refer to an insect wing folded back on itself. From the Latin plicare, to fold, also replicare, to unfold or to reply. An answer as an unfolding. To speak, for instance, to a figure with wings, and then to see the wings begin to unfold, as your answer. As in, "I love you," and she unfolds her wings to leave you.

I tried drawing her and am no artist. I filled a book, and then another.

Replicatory can mean, "of the nature of a reply."

. . . .

Káthodos, or, Original Sin

Descent of the soul, the fall; the fear of fallenness: "*Hester Panim* is connected by some modern thinkers to the notion of *tsimtsum*, God's self-limitation. If God overspills the universe, there is no room for humanity. Therefore, faced with this problem of theological physics, God withdraws." —David J. Wolpe

Of the Past, the Unspeakable

A kind of haunting hinders him—
no, me—during his day. Mine. This
current lingering on the line, Child,
electric, instigation enters,
or not…cows, for instance, walk
and eat simultaneous. Unhindered.
But do not speak.

What it means is, something
always hinders, someone, unless
a freeing like erasure lightens,
illumines, the path, the load.
To linger is to love. Live. Delay
departure till the cows
which cannot speak

191

come home. Clearly something
happened here. Cleverly. He had
"fair-feathered feet," not I. No eye
in that, there, to witness. Ill-formed
offspring of my feeble brain,
she said. Not me. Mine. This
speaking is all…

however, to hover this way above
the page like pasturage is
to feel filled pleasantly
unformed past or passion. To speak
is to wait for better weather,
to watch. Forget and fasten
to space opened there, thereby.

Repose

The tractrix is the evolute of the catenary,
these names of curves being what we love…
geometry becomes us, our essential sadness

such as *asymptote*—aligning
the unbearable vision with bearable
desire, a kindness of geometry.

"Catenary" was invented in the Age of Reason,
the word and the concept, but not the shape. Or yes,
a shape can be invented. From Latin *catena* "*chain*"

the name *tractrix* was coined ("Coin" from the Latin
cuneus, wedge, then cornerstone, (not to mention the vulgarism)
then die (as in, device for stamping a coin))(the path

of a word trailing along a horizontal history) by Huygens,
who also invented the clock. Imagine a boy pulling
a stone on a string, the string a little longer

than the distance from the boy's hand
to the sidewalk. The stone bounces a bit
on the concrete, makes a satisfying clatter,

background noise to the boy's thinking,
if thinking is the word—something more like
reflecting, from the Latin, "to bend."

His mind was bending, as if to the magnetic field
of earth, the very earth. The mind a magnet.
Any boy or girl would bend. That clock had a pendulum,

a weight on a string, like a stone to touch to try
to touch the earth the desire of each for each,
stone to earth. A distinction allows *sensuous*

to be about touch, as in the stone at rest
a sensuousness of stone, grave, of earth;
allows *sensual* to be of sex... *sensuous*

invented by Milton (1641), an attempt
to avoid the sexual overtones of *sensual*.
Somewhere must be other forms of desire,

other shapes than sexual. Pointless, maybe,
the distinction. In "Figure Drawing for All"
Andrew Loomis described (in words) before drawing

the reclining female nude, how the parts
of a body which can move will assume prettier poses
than in their upright modes. Shapes assemble into

larger shapes, lines linger into lyric. Pendular
parts draw the weak mind of the boy in the night
who has no other object to align, who leans

over the borrowed book in moonlight.
I used to live in a body. I now am that body,
not inhabitant. An intricate intrigue...imagine a people

wander the hillsides at whim, urge flocks
to wander with them, follow seasonal
impulses. The people are the landscape, as are

animals and plants and air and sidewalks.
The study of the tractrix started with a problem
posed to Leibniz: *What is the path of an object dragged*

along a horizontal plane by a string of constant length
when the end of the string not joined to the object moves
along a straight line in the plane?   —*Famous Curves Index*

ACKNOWLEDGMENTS AND NOTES

"Theory of Mind" (ToM) … is better looked at as an assemblage of diverse skills for relating one's own action to those of others. Thus different creatures may have different potentials for ToM, and the particular bunch of ToM skills exhibited by a group of humans may reflect their history perhaps even more than their biology."
    —Michael Arbib, "The Mirror System Hypothesis. Linking Language to Theory of Mind" (http://www.interdisciplines.org/coevolution/papers/11)

Anomalies of Water

The writings of Barry Mazur were crucial to this collection, especially in "The Twelve Symmetries," and "How It Feels, and Why," which also uses language from "Supervision 2: Somatic Sensation and Pain," (http://www-staff.psychiatry.cam.ac.uk/~dew22/supervisions/#list).

"Anomalies of Water" uses language from Martin Chaplin, (http://www.lsbu.ac.uk/water/anmlies.html).

Language in several poems was taken from Christopher Smart, (http://www.pseudopodium.org/repress/jubilate).

Grateful acknowledgment to:

Salt for publishing "Anomalies of Water," "Custody of the Eyes," and "How It Feels and Why"

Web Conjunctions for publishing "The Twelve Symmetries"

Zing for publishing "A Sort of Drowning a Slower Dance"

University of Denver Magazine for commissioning and publishing "Knowing Better"

Electronic Poetry Review for publishing "Was It Fallen It Was a Floating World, It Was Fallen Was It a Floating World," "Who Is Dying," and "Lies"

Columbia Poetry Review for publishing "Treatment Options."

"What Did You Make the Clouds Out Of?" was part of Joan Dickinson's installation "The Architecture of Honey," Illinois

State Museum Galleries in Chicago, Springfield, and Lockport, 2007-2009;

"The Twelve Symmetries" was part of a collaboration with Amanda Traxler.

Previously published books:

The Difference between Night and Day, Yale University Press, 1978.

White Monkeys, The University of Georgia Press, 1981.

The Language Student, Louisiana State University Press, 1986.

The Erotic Light of Gardens, Wesleyan University Press, 1989.

Massacre of the Innocents, The University of Iowa Press, 1995.

Wake, The University of Iowa Press, 1999:
> The poem "Wake" quotes from Shakespeare, "As You Like It," Robert Graves, *The Greek Myths*, Penguin, 1955, 170, y, and from John Milton, *Paradise Lost*, Book XI.

Airs, Waters, Places, The University of Iowa Press, 2001:
> "Against the Cycle of Saint Ursula (Carpaccio) uses language from Jacopo da Voraigine, *Golden Legend*, edited by Nicolo Malerbi, printed in Venice by Jenson, 1475, and from Walter Benjamin. The selection from "Echo" ends with the sounds of Latin first declension feminine plural endings.

Matter, The University of Iowa Press, 2004:
> "The Naming of Shadows and Colors" uses language from Philip Ball, *Bright Earth: Art and the Invention of Color*, Farrar, Straus and Giroux, 2001.

Tendril, Omnidawn Publishing, 2007:
> "Tendril" uses language from Christopher Smart and John Clare as well as from "Famous Curves Index," (http://www-groups.dcs.stand.ac.uk/~history/Curves/ Curves.html), and Gaisi Takeuti, *Memoirs of a Proof Theorist: Gödel and Other Logicians*, [translated by] Mariko Yasugi, Nicholas Passell. River Edge, N.J.: World Scientific, 2003.

Special thanks to Nic and Linda for inspiration, patience, and love; and to others whose work inspired and became part of my own: William Wiser, Cole Swensen, Donald Revell, and dearest friend Beth Nugent; to Richard Howard for encouragement, especially during the early years; much gratitude also to Malinda Markham, Maureen Owen, Joan Dickinson, Amanda Traxler, Vicki Hearne, Stanley Plumly; to the work of Barry Mazur (www.math.harvard.edu/ ~mazur/), and Philip Ball (www.philipball.com); and to Rusty Morrison and Ken Keegan.

Bin Ramke has written nine previous poetry collections. He holds the Phipps Chair in English at the University of Denver, and he also teaches on occasion at the School of the Art Institute of Chicago. In 1978, he was awarded the Yale Younger Poets Award. He grew up in east Texas and south Louisiana.

DISCARDED FROM
GARFIELD COUNTY
LIBRARIES